About the Author

Mark Sephton is a personal mentor to entrepreneurs. His mission to help others has seen him break into global markets while working with start-ups and millionaire entrepreneurs around the world. Mark's love for entrepreneurship has been expressed through serving as TV host of the show *One more round and hosting the Brainz Magazine Podcast*. When not on the big screen Mark is a regular contributor to entrepreneur magazine and a speaker for corporate events, entrepreneurship summits, and major conferences worldwide. His expertise in personal and professional development has positioned him as an expert in the industry, resulting in transformational experiences for audiences, clients, and businesses alike. Drawing from personal experiences, Mark has taken the essence of what he has experienced and built a business that helps draw out the magnificent potential that every person holds using his GPS system to highlight blind spots, efficiencies and deficiencies. He is also the author of two personal development books *Inside Job* and *Plot Twist*.

Dedications

My late grandfather Albert Haynes, a man who never hurt
me once and my three beautiful children Lois, Casey and
Eva who inspired me to be the best dad and man to them and
all that are around me.

Mark Sephton

MARK OF A MAN

Helping men become better men

AUSTIN MACAULEY PUBLISHERS™

LONDON • CAMBRIDGE • NEW YORK • SHARJAH

A CIP catalogue record for this title is available from the British Library.

ISBN 9781398454262 (Paperback)
ISBN 9781398454279 (ePub e-book)

www.austinmacauley.com

First Published 2021
Austin Macauley Publishers Ltd®
1 Canada Square
Canary Wharf
London
E14 5AA

Acknowledgements

My extremely supportive Girlfriend Anna who has always
been a huge advocate of my work.

Table of Contents

Foreword

I have had this book inside me for a long time, though the timing to start writing never felt right. I love to speak about my experiences, out of the rawness and vulnerability I am experiencing, because then I can really connect with you on an emotional level and that's really important because we are often told as men to not be emotional, to not really show what we really think and feel. Some of it is our upbringing and other parts could be culture or what society says is true or right for a man to behave and express. Men have to be strong and look like they have it all together. I have even been criticised for being too sensitive, for crying too much, for showing and telling people what's within me. I have even second guessed and had negative thoughts about myself, questioning is it right to just let it all out. After deliberating those thoughts and feelings and going through one extreme of thinking that the way I deal or don't deal with hardships is wrong I am now swinging the other way to educate and challenge people, in particularly men to own how they feel and be brave enough and vulnerable enough to let your deepest pains and hurt out, it's going to take courage, you may be judged for it and even ridiculed, but with the increase in mental health awareness especially amongst men, I need to really stir up a hope and show men a way out to express how they feel without feeling like they are less of a man, to educate men that actually owning those feelings makes you more of a man than you've ever been.

If you have read my book Inside Job, you will know the vulnerabilities and challenges I faced as a child. My adult life was for the most part something different, but on the back end of a divorce life left me feeling whipped, broken, hurt and struggling for breath. Trying to figure out what had gone wrong, what was wrong with me, to find and create a new normal, to know how to communicate effectively with those closest to me, knowing that my decisions always have the opportunity to impact on others, whom in the case of my children are very much an innocent part in the choices me and my ex-wife decided in separating. When you make a choice like that everyone has an opinion, even silence is an opinion of how people think and see the choices you make.

I want to acknowledge some of the pain that as men we feel deep within our very hearts. We all want to provide, we all want to achieve, we all want to protect and be strong. When a man doesn't feel like a man it renders him helpless, it destroys his self-esteem and worth. It takes him down paths that even he wants to desperately avoid.

I want this book to speak to your heart and to make men better men. To make men be brave and honest with how they feel. I will be brutally honest with some of the pain and doubts I have had within me. It won't always be pretty, but as I have said time and time again. Everything we go through isn't just about us, it's a lesson, a key, a hope to someone else's pain and fear. I want what I have experienced to help protect, strengthen and educate another man. That's what manhood is about, helping your fellow man. It can be a very lonely place being a man. We have totally different pressures to women.

While this book is focused for men, I am not trying to alienate women and I certainly won't be using this book to bash or belittle any woman, in fact the opposite. Helping and addressing men, I am hoping this book will help women, because let's be honest ladies, most men don't know how to behave let alone live.

Men do get a bad press, and rightfully and justifiably it's probably warranted at times, but if a man is to improve and grow and take up his rightful place, it's not going to help if he isn't given the room and space to grow, to take ownership and show his worth.

There is too much hate between men and women, far too much. We are both guilty. Men are guilty of treating women poorly and women are guilty of belittling and undermining the differences a man possesses within his heart and soul. We need each other.

I want to address the men; we need to treat women better. We need to listen, we need to honour and respect women and what they are and most importantly what's within them. We don't treat women right, I see the way most men look at a woman in the street and it's disgusting. I have seen the way men write to women via social media and it's disrespectful. A disclaimer here, have I always treated women in the right way, nope I haven't, but have I been man enough to say sorry and make every effort to put it right. Yes, I have.

I want to open the lid on the eternal challenges I have faced and yet have become an unspoken truth. I want men to get real, embrace the truth that we both feel and experience and find a way to heal ourselves and move forward.

We need to continue to be a voice and not an echo. We need to find our own voices, we do that by being one with ourselves. We become one with ourselves when we own all that we are, say and do. Let's take ownership for where we are at today and be brave enough to face our own demons and struggles.

While this book will have a certain focus of when going through a relationship break up, the principles and stories which I share are really equipped to educate and improve the way a man both thinks and expresses himself. A man being a man and a woman being a woman is a beautiful thing to see.

We live in a world where the world of equality has gone mad. Hear me right here, when it comes to things like pay a man and woman's income should be no different for doing a like-for-like job. However, the reality is men and woman are not actually equal, they are different, both sexes carry a unique skill set and framework which is to compliment the opposite sex, not to compete against it. Some things men do much better than women, and some things women do much better than men. I want to focus on what we men can do better and what a real man looks like. This is where "Mark of a man" comes from. What mark are you making as a man? What does your community need you to be? What does your family need you to be? Let's get real over the pages which are to come.

Chapter 1 - Failed Disappointment

We all brave the marks of disappointment. None come more deeper or painful than a divorce. I guess it's fair to say most people who get married don't plan on divorcing or separating. It does seem at least in the public eye that most marriages are failing even after a few years. I can't really celebrate the fact I was married for fifteen years, it still ended in a failed disappointment of a divorce.

While I am not prepared to talk about the details of why my marriage broke down, at the end of the day it takes two people to make it work and two people to make it fail, I am however prepared to tell you the hell I went through even after this decision was made that my marriage had come to the end of the road. It hurt like nothing I had experienced before, even if it was something I had decided needed to happen. You will know from my book "Inside Job" that I came from a broken family myself when I was a child. I battled for so long knowing I was going to be putting my kids through the potentially and difficult challenges of a mum and dad who loved them very much but who no longer lived under one roof and are no longer functioning as a typical normal family would.

In some ways me being sensitive to the pain and unrest I experienced when I was a child, I was proactive to protect them from the experiences I had and for the most part I feel I protected them from a lot of unnecessary feelings and pain by being able to preempt their thoughts and conclusions, I was swift to reassure them that this was not their doing, that it's not a reflection of my love for them, that the security they have with me is assured. I needed them to know without a shadow of a doubt that they were not responsible. I know I felt that way when my parents divorced, I think it's a natural thought to have so I tirelessly reassured them that this was not the case.

I also had to weigh the fact that when I got married I made a commitment before God. Me and my ex-wife agreed we didn't want to follow the sad patterns that both of our parents had experienced and we had numerous counselling sessions but fundamentally they didn't work. The reality being that the only way it could work was down to the two of us and for whatever reason we couldn't stop it going to where it did. It's hard to be honest with yourself and despite your efforts you can't find a way forward.

It's a hard weight to carry when you set your intentions and desires to something and your best isn't good enough. I don't feel guilt. I think we both recognised in the end that we were not helping each other and while it would be hellish going it alone, fundamentally it was for the good of both of our sakes.

You have to look within yourself and feel the depth and disappointment of something which you have invested so much of your time and energy into and for it to arrive at the point in which it did for both of us.

Sadly, you also experience what others feel about any decision you make in life. Typically I don't give too much credence to what others think, they only see through their own lens and experience. Though I must say, when your soul is ravished by such pain, the opinion of others seems to affect you more harshly. It's often what people didn't do or didn't say which spoke of their opinion and feelings towards such a decision. Yet the irony of when people play judge and jury in your life is they fall from grace to the challenges which rumble on behind closed doors themselves. At least I manned up to mine and made a decision for the sake of all rather than go through the motions and have years of regret.

Disappointment breaks a man's spirit. I have always been a family man. I have always loved the sense of family community and togetherness, to break that was heartbreaking. When your choices affect others it's a hard pill to swallow. Yet we each have our own life to live, one day my children will marry and will go through relationship problems, thankfully they will have two loving parents who will be there to support and give them reassurance and advice.

With time I realised that I never lost being a family man, it just looked different and I had to find a new way of being able to express myself to protect and nurture the relationships with my children and my closer family members. I have continued to see, invest and express many joyful moments with my children, taking them on little breaks to the seaside and having them stay with me every other weekend. I have always been focused on my family. I think at times when other relationships and dynamics within your family are more of a challenge it's very helpful to keep investing in the relationships that are working. I really wanted to focus a little more on my dear nephews. I love being an uncle and find that sometimes you have to be to others, which you hope one day others will be to you. My girlfriend loves being an aunty, and I felt challenged by her love and devotion to raise my game as an uncle to my precious nephews.

Being a family man to me is as much as being available and showing up than anything else. It's about investing your time and energy, it's about creating memories and going the extra mile. I turned my initial disappointment into reframing how I saw things and then decided to invest my time in lifting others up, there is no greater place to invest your time and love than in children.

In the dictionary the word disappointment means sadness or displeasure caused by non-fulfilment of one's hopes or expectations. We daily experience levels of disappointment. It means you care. It means you have a vested interest in something. We need to embrace that feeling and reflect on not just why we are feeling it but how we didn't meet that hope or expectation. We don't reflect to fall into a pity party, we reflect so we can own it and move beyond it. We have all felt the harshness of failed disappointment.

I reference disappointment for the sake of it being an emotion. Some people are raised it's not good to show emotion, or you need to curb your emotion. I don't agree, express your emotion, own it. I get a little ticked that doctors in particular are so quick to issue pills to those who are depressed. There is a time in our life that we should feel sad, disappointed and depressed if the route of that is justified. I want to tell each of you men that it's vital and it's important to show emotion. The shortest verse in the bible is "Jesus

Wept" Jesus showed emotion, a great role model of what a man should really reflect.

The gap between reality and our expectation is where disappointment sits. The gulf between the two is something I have felt so much these past few years. The visions and heart for where I want to be and whom I want to be, in relation to where I am now and who I am now.

Disappointment can actually be a lighthouse to what it is we really want, it can help us evaluate what's really important to us and what we are willing to tolerate or change in our life. It also helps us evaluate what we will accept with regards to the behaviour and beliefs of others and how they may or may not affect our inner world.

It's one thing to face the disappointment of what you may experience from others, people always have expectations of what we should or shouldn't do. I know divorce is not a popular route to take, I understand that, it's not pretty, it's not easy and sadly people do get hurt, but people equally get hurt if they stay in something which isn't healthy, happy or adding value or an experience of love. Divorce will always get a bad press and rightly so, but there are times when it's the only choice you have.

Dealing with your own disappointment is a slightly different ball game, when you are disappointed by the outcome or perhaps you may be disappointed in yourself, that can sometimes be the hardest thing to overcome and move past, we often get stuck in our own heads, we don't always find a quick way out. I know what I expect of myself, the reason relationships are hard is because you can't make the other person, say and do or think the way you do. You do however know how to affect those things for yourself. We are each responsible for our choices and decisions and perhaps when we reflect on them, we may at times feel we let ourselves down or we should have done better at a particular event in our lives.

When we reflect on our relationships we may find we let ourselves down. I had every intention of when I got married for that to be until death does me part but I never made it to that. That happens and you have to process and heal on the fact what you intended didn't come to fruition, you then tend to reflect on everything that may have led you to that point knowing you are at least half responsible for making a relationship work or not.

I know I am human, I know my vulnerabilities and my challenges as a man, I know what I am capable of both in the positive and the negative. I know my heart is good, I know I have good intentions and a spirit to do the right thing, I also know what it's like to disappoint yourself, to let yourself down, knowing you are capable of more or a better way of dealing with things.

It is clear that when we truly reflect on past disappointments that we use them for our greater good. I believe it's paramount that we flip the way we look at things. I have been mindful that too often we are looking at what we can get out of a relationship, when we are single we tend to look for the ideal woman (or man). We focus a lot of our energy on the woman we want and pay very little attention to the man (or woman) we need to be in order to attract such a partner into our life.

If I think specifically about the man I need to be to my girlfriend, I do draw some of those learnings from my failings as a husband in my previous marriage. One of the things I picked up in marriage counselling was this phrase "Entering into each other's world." Which really meant that when a woman speaks to you about something, even if you have no interest in the subject being discussed, you should react positively to it because what the woman is really saying is I want you to enter into my world because this is what is important to me, the worst thing we can do is be dismissive of what she is sharing or pay no attention to what is being said. I have experienced first-hand with my girlfriend that I have made huge progress in this area. She has many topics of interest, some I share and others I don't have a Scooby Doo what she is going on about, yet I immediately internalise she is asking me to enter her world, so I will listen and be happy and do my best to add something to the conversation, if I can't I will tell her to go speak to another friend about it so she can get her mental fix.

We need to be men who care, who create trust by listening, showing up and being mindful of our behaviour. Women value security and safety highly, they want to feel taken care of, not exposed, not embarrassed but safe. We need to be masculine in our energy, not aggressive but secure. Interestingly if you want a woman to express her feminine side it's very simple, be masculine. You need to lead but not dominate, be assertive but fair, accomplished but not proud. Think about who you need to be in your relationships in order to get out of them what you would like. If you want to attract an unbelievable woman you have to be an unbelievable man... I am sure you get my drift.

Here are a few ways to dealing with disappointment

- Acknowledgement is the first key to finding freedom from disappointment, own the fact it's there
- Have an honest conversation with yourself, accept your role and responsibility within the situation
- Give yourself grace, remind yourself you are human and take the learnings from the pain you feel
- Remember life doesn't always go to plan or indeed play fair
- Remind yourself how you feel is temporary and not permanent
- In reminding yourself that we only get disappointed over things we care about, accept that your heart was invested in the situation otherwise the emotional kick back of disappointment wouldn't be there.

Chapter 2 - Pressure

The pressure a man feels is unrivalled. Of course we all face pressure, we also each experience different pressures. As a man we face the pressure of providing, of carrying out expectations which are upon a man, to be strong, to not show weakness, to explore and to conquer. We also have the pressure of what people expect us not to be: vulnerable, fearful and uncertain.

Some pressures we put on ourselves, other times we allow society, our culture or our upbringing to overwhelm us with pressures. Of course women face pressures too, but the pressures are different. When a man feels like he can't fully express his manliness the pressure builds to breaking point. We don't feel like a man when we are unable to provide or when our ability to provide becomes limited. It's not just the pressure of being able to provide for ourselves and those around us which weighs a man down. Society creates this image of a man which in my eyes is a little warped or at the very least missing key components of what a man really should look like in terms of his character and personality. We are taught to be tough and physical and while I believe all men should have a masculine energy, not every man with strong muscles and aggression is the kind of man I want to be or indeed useful when the shit hits the fan. Too often there is far too much focus on the physical strength of a man that they suffer the malnourishment of a strong soul, clear mind and an honest spirit. If you are going to have the muscles make sure you have the quality and strength of a sound mind and character too. It's much better to be a man of strong character than of strong muscle, but the excellence of a man is in having them both. I see far too many men dedicated to their bodies or the gym than they are to the depth of their relationships or ambitions within the world of business or their career, often it's masking the pain and pressure we all face as men, which really comes down to the essence of being enough and measuring up.

Let me get real, right or wrong we have an expectation to not be helpless. You know something, over the past few years I have felt more helpless than ever before. Going through a divorce gives you an absolute kicking. Knowing my choices affected my kids and those around me, it felt whichever way I turned was going to cause pain to someone. The road ahead which ever I took was going to hurt, many nights I cried myself to sleep and I did feel helpless for my situation. I did want to give up, I never wanted to take my own life but I did want the pain and suffering in my heart to stop. The problem with divorce is not just the separation it's the fact that so much of your world changes all at once, the place you live, not waking up to your children being there day in and day out, the fact that you will never experience many things again as a family in one tight cohesive unit. Add to this the unknown of how everything will pan out, to try and create a new normal. It takes time, but I found that even the small things that normally I could bat off became overwhelming due to the mental state I was in, for example a friend missing my birthday, that happens but due to the helpless state I was in I reacted to that in a negative way. It felt like they didn't care, that I wasn't important.

The ideal that is projected is that men should not really show emotion, it's not normal or natural. What I will say is it's actually not the way God designed it to be, he wants men to express their emotions and understand what they mean. It's a massive part of who we are, If I encourage one man through this book to own his feelings and have the courage to express them the right way then hallelujah I am thrilled I have taken the time to communicate this with you. As men we must let the emotion out and not be ridiculed for it. Too many times I have felt ashamed or projected on as a man for being emotional, for showing tears, like there is something wrong with me. The problem isn't within me showing emotion it's in the history of the world which says a man must not show how he really feels because it's not acceptable and yet we see more mental health cases than ever before. There is more male suicide than female suicide and that's not a coincidence. Men are not encouraged to talk or express, they are told to suck it up and deal and yet the cracks are starting to appear.

As a man we are told not to be scared, anxious, depressed, tired, frustrated, vulnerable or lonely and yet I have felt each and every one of these emotions more than ever before. Does that make me less of a man? Nope. It makes me more of a man who is in tune with his emotions and that's a good thing. Express yourself, man! I do want to make a strong point here because this actually cheeses me off within the context of getting help from the medical profession. Doctors are far too quick to administer pills and medication rather than create a chance for men to talk and understand that when you go through hell it's okay to feel sad and depressed. If I didn't feel those things after a divorce then I am not human but a robot. Sometimes it's okay to feel like shit when you've been through exactly that. Alarm bells should ring if what we feel is totally unrelated to what we are experiencing, then perhaps medical intervention is then needed. It's not all bad if we each need some medical intervention from time to time to help us cope with our mental health challenges but let's not just reach for that when perhaps we just need to accept the pain we are going through because what we are going through actually hurts, you're supposed to be sad, means you care. Means you were not living a lie but you had invested time and energy into something which now has reached its end.

It is very useful to be able to map out your emotions, I often take pen and paper and write down the emotions I am feeling, it's very helpful to do this when you're in a high emotional state in the middle of a trauma or trigger where your reactions are intensified. Pay particular attention to what each emotion stands for. When I went through my divorce some of my emotions were disappointment, anger, sadness. You then have to think about what each of those emotions represents and means to you. If we take disappointment as an example we would understand that my emotion of disappointment would stem from the fact I never wanted my marriage to end in divorce, I may then need to explore why it did, or other aspects of that disappointment, for example what example have I left my kids. The reason you do this exercise is not just to acknowledge and understand the emotions you feel but more importantly why and what are they linked to.

Before we are able to go full circle on points of reflection and then growth we have to become far better acquainted at what we feel, then why we feel it. Once we have ascertained why and what, we then have to reassess our role and the position we need to work towards in order to release our emotions, find healing and then adjust to disappointment etc. We get to the self-improvement stage by going through this process, there is no escaping it, we want to heal but we also want to learn. We want to realise why we have the emotion, what that emotion means and then how to use it as part of our healing and then our re-set and finally our new form.

Once we've explored the disappointment it's important going forward into a new relationship or marriage that you quickly understand what the reasons are it failed in the first place. It's also vitally important that we deal with our own expectations when moving forward. Emotions come and they go, we have positive ones and negative ones and we need to understand what leads us to these experiences, can we reduce the route of the negative emotions by being mindful and attuned to not making the same mistakes and equally can we ramp up the behaviours and choices which result in high levels of positive emotions. Never lose sight of the fact that emotions are always moving which is encouraging when you don't feel great and humbling if you do.

Emotions will never knock you too far off course if you have a clear and healthy view of who you really are, because who you are doesn't change so rapidly and repeatedly like emotions, your grounding comes from who you are with yourself. Meaning who are you to yourself. This is so key to really finding grounding in your foundations and ensuring you have a lifetime of personal growth and not just circumstantial growth, sometimes we grow based on outcomes we don't choose, but we can grow from all things if we are clear and intentional about it.

It's so important when you go through something like a divorce that you redefine your new self that you spend important energy on who you are to you. Start doing the things you love, start to express yourself, start to build and do the things which resonate with you. When I moved into my new apartment it was like a blank canvas, I could design, style and form each room to my liking and taste, it was a hugely important moment but also stood as a metaphor for the chance to start over, while starting over isn't always fun, most things are about how you frame them in your mind. Some people see hassle and frustration in starting over, others like myself see an opportunity to have and be and do all the things I wanted to do but never did them for whatever reason.

We manage the pressure of others and ourselves by constantly redefining who we are, committing to those things which resonate and strengthen your authenticity which gives you purpose and vigour to keep showing up and keep turning up every time you get out of bed.

How to deal with pressure:

– Give yourself time to think, adjust and assess
– If what you are facing is time sensitive then make a choice which is in-line with your core values
– Be creative in your thinking and don't be afraid to ask for help
– Shift your environment even if it's for ten minutes, it's amazing what a change of scenery can do for your mood and your perspective

- Understand that we all face pressures on a regular basis, make choices that if they were made public you would be happy with them
- Break it down, don't be overly consumed by the detail, focus your energy on one part of the problem
- Give yourself a time out, it's not wrong to ask for more time if you have the ability to do so

Chapter 3 - Expectation

As a man we have a great expectation which is placed upon our shoulders. Expectation derives from society, our culture, our upbringing, our family and friends and most of all ourselves. We each have an expectation of how we should behave, perform and live. These expectations are what others put on us and also what we put on ourselves. The challenge for each of us is which expectations to rise up to and meet and which ones do we either ignore or dismiss from those around us and the small voices within us.

Expectations can be both helpful and hindering. Helpful in the sense that we have clear guidelines, this could be in the form of our conduct or even our duty to take responsibility for something. Hindering when others have an expectation in which we can't meet, don't want to meet or don't know how to meet it.

Fundamentally I believe we must count the cost of expectation upon ourselves first and then from there decide to accept the expectation people or society place on us in order to measure up or perform to a level which is expected.

We can all go back to our school days where our form tutor or teacher would evaluate our performance and our behaviour, this is measured by what the school expects from its pupils but also what our teacher expects from us, as they are equipped to educate. Often as I am sure the majority of you probably experienced on your report cards or hearing these words during a parents evening during your school years "Mark must do better," "Mark can do better." It's clear even from a young age that we have an expectation of what is expected of us. How quickly we can read or write, how we behave through a lack of manners or in some cases good ones.

We live throughout our life with the weight of expectation firmly on our shoulders. If we consider what "Man" is expected of him in the twenty-first century we would probably think of some of these thoughts, "He is to provide for his family, he is to protect and shield his family both physically and emotionally, he is to be a gentleman and ensure the safety and wellbeing of all others is put ahead of himself." I do believe that these are a few things that men, all men should take ownership for and step up to the plate.

This book is to help men be better men. Before we can meet the expectation of others, we firstly must meet the expectation of ourselves. Have you ever pondered and considered this question, "What do I expect of myself?" Expectation can be found in our beliefs, our behaviour and our performance, it is found in the way we treat strangers and how we treat our loved ones.

It's often a very bitter pill to swallow when we don't meet the expectation of others, but we must first frame what we expect of ourselves. I can go first and be a little vulnerable here.

I expect of myself to be responsible for all of my actions, even those that I maybe not proud of or can share a thousand reasons why I acted or behaved or performed in a certain way, we can all find excuses and justifications for why we let ourselves down or others. Fundamentally I expect myself to constantly grow, to own my mistakes, to have the courage to admit when I was wrong and the humility to say I am sorry. I have apologised at times to my children, I think it's important we show children how to own up to our own failings, to have the humility to ask for forgiveness and move on. I am not interested in feeling guilty or making others feel guilty. We are all human and fall short. When the tone of my voice has upset one of my children it's important to me that I take responsibility for that and offer an apology if it's necessary.

I have a huge expectation upon my shoulders to ensure my children learn from my mistakes and all that is good in me I leave and invest within them. So when I leave this earth it's not what I leave for them which is going to be the biggest influence on their life, but rather what I leave in them. I have an expectation upon myself to be the best dad I can be, I am their father chosen by God to impart all wisdom, success and understanding to their hearts and minds, while also protecting them from my failings and shortcomings so they don't repeat mistakes I have made.

If you are not a father the same principles apply, people are watching how we act and behave all the time, you could be an uncle, brother or partner and each relationship comes with a form of expectation and responsibility. We need to accept that we have a part to play in society. I get so appalled by the conduct of some men, the way they speak about a woman isn't cool, it isn't charming and it shouldn't have a place in society but sadly it does. Women deserve respect and if we start to respect women the way they deserve we may find that they love us better and don't give us the hard time that sometimes we probably deserve. As men we need to take the first step, it's the gentlemanly thing to do.

We can no longer afford to be clumsy or brain dead in the way we relate to others especially women. I am nauseated by the lack of class in the way some men speak of women and also the way they look at a woman. When I say "look" I actually mean it two-fold, looking in the sense of how they perceive a woman and also the way they physically look at a woman, sadly most men are not subtle and if I was a woman and saw a man look me up and down and crane their neck to keep looking I would feel pretty uncomfortable and I see men do that all the time, it's not cool, its actually creepy and doesn't create the right impression for a woman or make her feel secure and safe. Don't do that. Be a gentleman in both your conduct and speech. Women love a gentleman, courteous and thoughtful which creates a sense of safety and security.

We all need a compass, a compass which defines our own expectation. We need to become clear on what our expectations are as a man and then measure them with our current performance and understanding. This has to be the first step, way before we consider the expectations others put on us, we must have our own understanding to get a clear view of how things really look. As a man we each have our own lens of seeing, thinking and interpreting. I imagine it will be most helpful for me to outline what my expectation of myself is and sharing a little about what my lens of expectation may look like, we may each have a few altering views with plenty of cross overs. There is not just one way to be a man but the essence and core of a man I believe should have some very familiar and similar features and characteristics.

When I mention we all have our own lens it's important to really grasp what I am getting at here, it was one of the significant revelations I became aware of with my psychologist. We all look at everything through this lens of understanding, every situation, problem, threat, opportunity, relationship, communication the whole nine yards. When I take someone's behaviour and put it through my lens of understanding or the way I see things I then make a judgement or interpret what that means. The biggest problem in doing this is very simple, we often mis-read or misunderstand someone's behaviour if our lens of understanding is different to theirs. For example, whenever I have my children I tend to hear less from my girlfriend, So I put this situation through my lens and I could only interpret negative responses and understanding as to why this could be, eventually we talked it through and I couldn't have been more wrong in my interpretation. The real reason why my girlfriend was more quiet when I had my kids was because she believed it was important that I be present with them and her way of loving me was giving me the space and energy to focus on them and not be distracted by herself. Her dad was always her hero and she valued so much her time with her dad that she wanted to ensure my children had the same experience that she did. Wow. Talk about misunderstanding a situation because my lens interpreted something very different.

Anyways I don't want to lose you here, we all have a lens of understanding, it may not always be right, it may need to be changed or adapted and it may not always serve you, but it's very helpful to know that we each have a different lens which means sometimes you may do something and it be misunderstood or interpreted in a different way to how it really is, it's important you know why you feel, think and understand the way you do and be comforted that not everything you do which may get a bad press is actually bad but it's more about the difference in the way each of us see things.

As I said the first step with expectation is you becoming clear on what you expect from yourself. As a man we may be a husband, boyfriend, father, daddy, partner, brother, uncle, son and friend. We have a responsibility. I want to prioritise the important people in my life, that means I expect to put those people before my work, for the most part I feel I do that. I want to be ever present and available to those I love, my relationships are really the most important thing to me, way above accomplishments or impressive accolades, I judge myself on my relationships and I also find that my relationships are what determine my general happiness and mood.

We must ensure that we meet our own expectations before we meet the expectations of others. I do not need to report in to anyone but myself and God about the choices I make and the way I conduct myself. While I have expectations on my relationships and they seem a focal point to the expectations I believe a man should accept, we also need to have an expectation with regards to the thoughts we have. That may look something like "I expect my thoughts towards others to be charming, kind and uplifting." As men we need to bring back that protective, honouring and kind way of speaking to others, focusing special attention to women and children in the way we speak about them, we need to step into our role and be a pillar of strength and comfort and let the words we speak over people be empowering, secure and create a positive impression.

The expectation of others or how we perceive what they think about us or indeed say about us can be a messy and difficult process and I have shared first-hand how I interpreted something very different to what my girlfriend was actually meaning. There is a difference between what we think we see and what we know. We have to be acutely aware and tuned in that some of the expectations we feel from others maybe more about what we think we see rather than what is really known about a situation. Once we know our own expectations we can then start to entertain the complexities of what others expect from us, but at no point should we lose our own compass and values as to the very minimum we expect ourselves to be as men. We must also be mindful to not mis- read by what we think we see in a situation and learn to talk things through to get a greater understanding of what actually is required or expected.

It's worth me reiterating this point but none of us can always meet the expectation of another, partly because we are human and partly because all our lenses are different, whose lens is right or wrong is not up for debate, we must ensure that our lens works within our own belief system and the fruit of our lens should manifest in sound choices which then produce a great result. It's helpful to know in some cases that regardless of how you interpret something, if someone's truth is different to yours then you don't need to be offended or try to make sense of everything, in some ways that's futile, because it doesn't always matter what it looks like through your lens if the other person's lens is completely different.

Be clear on what you want and expect from yourself, we can't always know what another person wants and it's impossible to please everyone, create your own compass, your own expectation and consistently deliver on that.

How to deal with expectations:

- If someone's opinion or desire for you is not in-line with what you want, let it go
- The old classic of under promise and over deliver is kept to giving yourself a break and reaping the rewards
- Realise the way you see you and the way others see you is different, if you can look in the mirror and feel at peace with yourself and your choices nothing else matters
- Sometimes it's helpful to talk through someone's expectations especially in a relationship, it's good to know what the other person is expecting from you, you can then decide if you can and or want to meet it
- If you have a high but healthy expectation of yourself it's less likely you won't meet the expectation of others
- Realise that you can't please everyone
- Remember you are growing daily, we don't stop growing which means at times we may fall short and that's okay.

Chapter 4 - Emotion

We are currently entering the fourth month of a UK lockdown due to the Corona virus sweeping the nation and our world. It's been a brutally difficult time for most of us. Many have said we are in the same boat, the reality is we are not in the same boat but in the same storm.

Whenever we personally go through something of course there is someone somewhere in the world who has it harder than ourselves, even so it does not minimise our own pain and suffering and we especially shouldn't minimise someone else's challenge or difficulty because we know someone else who is going through something even more painful than ourselves.

My boat looks very different to yours. Quite frankly I have personally struggled over these three to four months because very little is pleasing to me, very little is my choosing. Do I understand the measures that have been taken by the British government and why they have been taken, absolutely! I appreciate that this virus can be deadly and it has ravished our nation with over 40,000 deaths and counting. Do we all need to be responsible with our hygiene and take actions to stop the spread? Yes, we do. However, I would have hugely benefitted from being able to make more personal choices while being sensible because my mental health as I am sure it's true for you too has taken a battering in trying to work things out by myself. Being so cut off and alienated isn't something which is fun or helpful regardless of the reasons why.

I live by myself, I get some relief when my children come and stay with me on the weekends but during the week it's a lonely place at times and the four walls are silent and cold. I would never in a million years choose to be isolated and cut off like I have been.

I do not need a high level of space or time to myself to function. To some introverts this would be heaven, to me whom is an extreme extrovert this hurts my very soul. I love human connection.

Emotions often come with some negative stigma. We may hear comments like "Emotions get you in trouble" and yes sometimes they do, but some things are worth the trouble if they are grounded in your own values and it does not break moral etiquette or criminal law.

I have had all the emotions you can think of over these few months, I have felt, anger, frustration, disappointment, loneliness, isolation, abandonment, sorrow, grief, loss, trauma, pain, confusion and many more painful and so-called negative experiences. I come from the world of positivity, I mentor clients on self-leadership. Yet it really is frustrating when many other experts and or coaches try and push those emotions away and tell you to decide about what your outlook is. While that is helpful at certain points if you're sat there with your leg blown off, don't tell me to be positive in that moment and think at least I have one good leg. I hate that kind of response, where is the empathy? It's important to acknowledge all emotions and stages of life.

The important thing here is to remember that there is a difference between sitting in your suffering and wallowing in it. I want to tell you that I personally believe it's okay to not be okay, it's okay to feel those emotions I have felt, what isn't okay is to wallow in them and never move out from those feelings. I don't want to stay there because they don't serve me. However they are there for a reason. We have God-given emotions for a reason, we all do. They are not innately bad. They are what make us human, they are what makes us relatable, compassionate and empathetic.

This world is more affected by emotional pain than it is affected by physical pain. I would actually go further and say the majority of our physical ailments and sicknesses derive from emotional pain which manifests in our body.

It is so important as men that we understand that emotions are normal and safe and don't need to be hidden to protect or promote our masculinity. We have allowed ego to dominate our own lives and I can see the damage ego from males in power has caused untold trouble and heartache to many.

We need to be better men, but the first step in being a better man to others is to be a better man to ourselves. We must start owning our own feelings and start being curious as to what they are and why they are there. Men stereotypically bottle their emotions up. I am not like most men, I would say over the last two years I cry once or twice a week. A part of that is because emotionally I have been through some traumas from my divorce and reliving my own parent's divorce when I was a child and having to be mindful about how now my own children must be feeling and how they are processing this life change.

Life is brutal at times. I have always said and captured this point in both my books "Plot Twist" and "Inside Job" the hardest road is always the one that goes through the core of whom you are (Heart).

I am extremely good at solving problems. I enjoy it, I love thinking on my feet, I love finding solutions. I think sometimes people think I don't realise the size or the reality of the problem, it's not true, it's just that I choose to put my energy and my focus on the solution. It's the same with Corona, some have said "Mark, you're not taking it seriously enough." It's not true, I have done everything I have been supposed to e.g. keeping the two metre social distance, washing my hands, wearing a mask, I just believe I am so sick and tired of feeling low in mood because most of the things I enjoy doing I cannot do right now and that isn't easy. I can't watch or play football, I cannot go out for a meal at a restaurant. I can't hug my family (Kids of course I can and do). I cannot see people the way I like to see them. I can't travel. My support network has been destabilised. All the natural things we all do to cope and give balance to our lives are now on hold.

So I am left with me and my emotions. Emotions are not bad, they can be complicated and sometimes they can get you in trouble but I realised what makes me the most happiest is when I allow my heart and not my head to rule my choices and alongside that my gut which is the umpire of peace based on my faith in God which helps me make decisions which resonate with my path and values.

As men we need to know it's okay to have emotion and even more importantly it's okay to show it, it does not mean you're weak, it's actually the opposite, being able to express is a sign of strength. I don't keep things locked in, one of the ways I express emotion is simply by talking. When I talk I process, when I process I can shift through my emotions, I can go from sitting in my negative emotion to then watching it disperse as I gain clarity.

The important thing to note with emotion is to allow it to have its place. Just don't start wallowing for days on end because then you will drown and it will bury you. Honour the pain, feel it and then let it leave.

You know something it's okay to be depressed at times, it's not strange if you go through a breakup or you lose a loved one or you get fired from your job, it's no wonder you feel depressed. There are times when I almost feel like you should be depressed if the situation is deserving of it, just don't stay depressed. We want you well, we want you to come through the healing process, but it is a process and that doesn't start with denial, it starts with acceptance.

You don't need antidepressants when you go through shit, you need time to heal and process. It's okay to not be okay.

Talking things through always helps me express my emotion, be mindful of the people or person you decide to journey some of these painful experiences with. I started working with a psychologist after identifying three behaviours which I couldn't seem to master even though I know what they are and what injury they cause me and in some cases what issues that may cause difficulties for others.

I practice what I preach. It's no good me mentoring people around self-leadership if I am not taking leadership and support from others. I realised that if I could heal myself I would, if I could fix myself I would because if it doesn't serve me and actually creates problems in my life I want it gone. So

I decided that I knew what my injuries were and that I needed to seek out someone who could help me, someone who could soothe me and give me the empathy but also the intervention of tools which I couldn't quite grasp for myself. Are the negative and painful emotions still there? Yes they are, but am I responding differently to things that trigger me and put me into threat mode, yes I have started that journey but it won't come over night. I want change and I want healing. Like with all things it's a process, changing the way we react to experiences isn't easy.

I have noticed, specifically this year of 2020 that my greatest lesson in personal growth and self-leadership has really fallen between the places and power of narratives. What I mean by that is the narrative I play out in my own head, in other words the story I tell myself based on what I experience and also interpret. We can all internalise each and every experience and each and every encounter, we formalise our own opinion based on what we tell ourselves. I have realised that the narrative in which I play out in my head has the ability to really determine the emotions I feel and these emotions then continue to determine my feelings and my choices. I have a tendency to want to take responsibility and hold myself accountable to everything I feel, but my growth and something you also need to be mindful of because it may well be a great source of breakthrough for you as it was for me, is that often what is projected towards us, or how we are treated by another actually has very little to do with you and I and everything to do with the one who is expressing it towards us.

We must have and find the ability to face and look at each narrative we find ourselves being governed by, we need to pause and be extremely intentional about how, what and why we are internalising some of the stories we play out in our heads. I know I have caused myself pain by choosing poorly the narrative I play out in my head depending on the events and relationships at play. We must face those thoughts and we must have the courage to look at them and empower ourselves and give ourselves permission to not take responsibility for each and every negative outworking. Continually ask yourself the question if you can reframe the story and narrative you play in your head, often we get caught spinning our own disk over and over again and wonder why the feelings stay the same. Ask yourself, can I look at this situation or relationship differently, is it really about me or is it about them. Reframing has protected me from myself, when I have chosen to internalise a situation which reflects badly about me, my value, my personality, my skill, my likability and yet in truth we don't need to be the one under the spotlight and beat ourselves up. So pause for a moment and ask yourself the question. Can I reframe my thoughts, can I reframe my narrative? I know first-hand that is much easier said than do, I have caused myself great heartache and pain when I have taken something personally which in reality was nothing about me. Being real is knowing the difference between what we perceive is true and what is actually true.

While identifying and reflecting on emotions, it's so important and yet also essential we answer to the emotion even if it's painful, we need to not only acknowledge it, we also need to communicate with it and address it, emotions will come and go and often over time they can take care of themselves, but like with most fires you can let them burn through their own course, or it's often more prudent and savvy to not continue to let the fire have free reign and stop it in its tracks, being a good steward especially when something has the ability to be destructive is wise and advantageous. Once you address the emotion you can circle back around and ask yourself is there the possibility that if I change my narrative it will change the feeling and in turn the feeling will change the way we feel about it and then the choices we make moving forward. Emotions are a good thing, if we learn how to relate to our emotions better, with more grace and ownership we may find some of the greatest lessons of personal growth are around the corner.

How to deal with emotions:

- Firstly remember emotions are not bad, they are God given, they are a feeling on how we are experiencing something in our life at any moment
- Find the right environment to express them, some emotion needs to be released behind closed doors, other times you may need a friend or a therapist to help you process
- Remember feelings and emotions come and go, they can't always be relied on to make life-long decisions.
- Give yourself permission to feel and experience different emotions without feeling guilty or bad, we are human.
- Get comfortable with voicing how you feel, it's more manly to know what you feel and have an ability to express it rather than to suppress it.
- Realise that there is more male suicide than ever before, life can sting and it's very important you have a support network where you can process and journey some of life's cruel events.

Chapter 5 - Pain

Pain is something we all experience, as a child I think I associated pain only with a physical condition but it seems as we all move into adulthood, the greatest pain is not so much physical but more emotional. We often associate trauma with some war-time event. We associate trauma often with those who have fought on the battlefields of war and see blood shed before their very eyes. Now trauma is much more prevalent in our hearts and our minds and not just exclusively in our body.

Pain is the bodies way of telling us something is wrong, something is misaligned, something is missing or broken or injured. A divorce for example is a type of emotional trauma, the breakup, the separation and the impact it has is not only felt by you but your ex-partner, children, wider family, friends and the wider community.

As men we don't always like to express our feelings or reveal how we feel because it's deemed "not manly" and yet I know women who are starting to express that they like a man who is emotionally intelligent and able to articulate his feelings, understand them and the feelings of others. Men struggle with this shift because it's often how we are raised or how society has informed us, stigmas like "emotions need to be kept quiet", or "a real man doesn't cry" are imbedded in man's history and yet I never believe for one second man was not to show and express emotion. If you have children like I do, it's important my kids know it's safe to feel the way they do and be able to express it without judgement or fear that they will be punished or belittled because of it.

Pain needs to be acknowledged. Whatever you do, do not sweep it under the carpet. Do not be avoidant of what you are feeling, honour it and give it its place to be felt and then gently move through that pain and enter healing and reflection and finally growth.

We have all faced pain, some of us on a daily basis. One of the biggest pains I face more often than not is the pain of absence. I am sure you can relate, it's the absence of the things you once had, could be a past relationship, or the death of a loved one, it could be your health or your dream job. Whatever it is for you, it causes pain because we are not supposed to be cut off from those things that are good and healthy for us and yet we all accept at some point it's a part of life. Even accepting isn't always easy and a sense of loss can still be very present even in accepting the way a situation of circumstance is.

I want you to know it's perfectly okay to hurt. It's okay to not be okay as I have already said. What isn't okay and I say this for the good of you is wallowing in self-pity and heartache indefinitely. It's okay to sit in your pain and hurt for a period of time, just don't stay there. The only way out is through, which means acceptance, then reconciliation within ourselves, we then find a resolve and a greater understanding, we take responsibility for our part, forgive ourselves and others if necessary and get back up, dust yourself down and go again.

I have often heard the phrase "It's not how you start but how you finish which matters." There is a lot of truth to that. While we have air in our lungs and blood pumping around our bodies we have an opportunity to move away from pain and gain ground.

Covid has brought pain to many people, in some ways more obvious than others, some have lost their lives or the lives of their loved ones, others have seen the stress of their spouse who is a doctor or nurse in extreme pressure during these months as they try to provide medical help to many inflicted by this horrible virus.

For others like myself it's been the removal of my support network which is a mix of activities and people. I haven't been able to play football in months, haven't been able to go to the cinema, haven't been able to hug my friends, haven't been able to travel. The lockdown has caused great pain to me and others alike, what makes it worse is that it feels when life is tough and some of those activities like playing football help you get through a tough time, you don't even have the option to escape reality even if it's for a few hours breather. Life is out of balance and it's become tricky even for the strongest amongst us.

We all need some time out, time out from ourselves and from the constant feelings of pain. Often people turn to addictions to mask the pain, it's obvious why many hit the drink in order to distract or numb them from reality. Some have taken their own lives because the pain has become unbearable.

While I have never had suicidal thoughts during my divorce, I very much wanted God to take me because the pain felt so great, life didn't make sense, the pain it was causing my children and all those affected it didn't seem my life was worth it. I just wanted the pain to stop. I know what pain is, I cried every day for six months straight during that time. I wept and even now on occasions something may trigger me which leads me to tears.

It's important you give yourself the space to grieve. We all are experiencing loss in some way. It's not manly to just keep it in, it could even make you sick. Confide in your partner or a dear friend and allow them to walk through the journey with you. I was thankful to have a few dear friends who helped me walk out my dark days but let's be honest, some of the paths me and you have to walk nobody else can walk with us, it's during those moments when everyone is sleeping and you get into bed and feel the reality and relive all the moments which break your heart and you look around and you are all by yourself, it's a sobering and humbling moment.

While social media is bittersweet I came across a statement which resonated with me so deeply during this time of lockdown. "Sometimes, what feels like punishment is actually preparation. Trust the plan, not the pain." Lockdown has caused me pain, separation from the people and the things I loved has stunk and I have hated it, simply because I don't get to choose, it's a beautiful thing to have options, when options are taken away it causes injury. If I take on board what this statement says its re-frames the way I think and the lens in which I see a situation. I probably don't want to hear it right now because I still feel very much in the lockdown and I would never have chosen the last three months but what happens if rather than me seeing it as a punishment because that's really how it has been feeling and I flip it to the fact perhaps this is preparing me for something greater then I feel I can take that pain and put it to some sort of good use.

We need to understand our responses to pain, the three-step process is important to remember when we are seeking change and to navigate life's current challenge. Firstly we must feel the emotion, in this case pain, we need to acknowledge it is present and indeed why it's present. We must know and become very acquainted with knowing what we feel and why we are feeling it, the second step to feeling the emotion of pain is indeed to express it, we need time to let it out, it's not always pleasant or easy to express something which may be attached to shame or guilt or embarrassment. The main thing in expression is finding the time and then the right environment to express that which you feel, at times that maybe more appropriate when you are by yourself and other times the burden and weight of the pain maybe needed to express itself with the help of a professional or a personal friend or connection.

Once we have felt the pain and then allowed ourselves to express it, we must then respond to the pain and anguish which is the most crucial and yet probably the hardest step of the three. The reason why it's the hardest is we have become accustomed to burying what we feel or hiding it is because of the shame and fear attached to it. We rarely want to respond to it but that is such a necessary component to moving beyond the pain and into healing. Everything we go through has its part, it's part of the ecosystem of the life we each live. Our response can come in the way of understanding the contrasts between the beauty and the brutality, the high and the low. The good times in contrast to the bad times are what give us context and help soothe our fears by remembering that better times will come.

When I was at the point of feeling my pain, I called it by name, I named it, I vocalised that I was in pain with my dear and closest friends and family. I told them I was hurting, I expressed that pain through tears, sometimes it was through a shout, other times it was through exercise. The pain within must be released otherwise like all negative emotions, if they are not expressed they can manifest in your body as sickness, which none of us want to experience. I did find myself crying and releasing my pain through tears, sometimes the shift was significant, other times my tears just seemed to leave me with a headache and emotional exhaustion, I am not sure why there was such contrast in how I felt but I trust the process of letting go, I gave myself permission to cry, I gave myself permission to seek help, to confine in help, I let the pain have its space and I expressed it.

I eventually responded to the pain with acceptance for what was, and acceptance for what was to come, acceptance was one part of my response. It's important to not lose sight of the other more positive aspects of life around you, it's never all bad and it's never all good. My response was, that over time it would pass, that gratitude would continue to help me not lose sight of those areas in my life which were still working even in the midst of struggle and difficulty. I also started to walk each and every day, I would start my day with an hour's walk to frame my mind and sharpen my mood. Action is the quickest way to shift emotion, action quietens the mind. The pain started forcing me to act, discomfort motivated me to change. It's not fun to cry day after day for six months straight, you have to take yourself away from the focused negative energy you can feel and reframe it into a season of your life that you're currently going through.

As I began to walk, as I began to focus on projects within my work and personal life, things started to settle and a balance of my emotions became much more rounded, as things settled I could think and act more clearly and wisely and over time I managed the pain and then it slowly but surely transitioned to healing and then peace and now I can see and feel a scar, a story of what took place and how that scar now represents healing and a new beginning while acknowledging the highs and lows we all face in life.

How to deal with pain:

- Give yourself time to heal
- Go get help, I have been into personal development for the past fifteen years and have been mentoring on it for the past ten, only this year did I start working with a psychologist, if you're hurting get some help
- Acknowledge the pain it's showing you something is off, don't ignore it, sit in it but don't wallow in it, accept it is there for now but with time it will pass
- Find out what soothes you, for me that maybe a massage, lighting candles, seeing my children, playing football, have a list of ten things which soothe you during times of pain
- Talk it out, so so important that we start becoming comfortable with talking things through

Chapter 6 - Fear

Fear rears its head in many many forms. Fear cuts off our supply of power. Fear is a common adversary. It can control our thoughts and dictate our choices if we let it. I do my level best to not allow fear to dictate my choices or indeed my decisions. I want to make decisions out of love. I don't want to be forced to do something because it may or may not happen.

We face fears every day in all shapes and sizes. Often our fears are not rational. Our fears are often not even logical, they can be the fear of something physical or can be the fear of something emotional, a fear of mistakes is the biggest fear that people are faced with.

We have to be honest about our fears in order to firstly live with them and then serve them notice. One way to deal with fear is exposure therapy. This isn't the most comfortable of therapies and often feels like you are losing control by actually exposing yourself to the fear.

I hate blood, most specifically my own. It was very common for me to pass out after cutting myself or even having a nosebleed. It's one of the most horrible experiences when everything goes cold, you go super faint and you pass out. I try to talk myself around, I remind myself that we are all made up of blood so it's inevitable if I cut myself then blood will be present but I can't move beyond my reaction. I am not there yet, but the more times I have a blood test or something requiring me to witness my own blood I feel a little stronger but I have certainly not mastered it.

The idea of exposure therapy is for me to keep being exposed to my fear and in doing so lessening its grip on me, the biggest problem is holding yourself in that place where in reality it's the last place you want to be.

I do not overly like anything to have power over me and seems to be one of the areas of my life where I have looked to find some release from. We often don't want to face our fears so we allow them to dictate the choices we make and our minds go into fight or flight where we may make choices that prevent the realisation of that fear manifesting. While I salute and believe it's noble to give blood at this moment I have not been able to do that. The proudest moment I have of me remotely overcoming this fear was with the birth of my son. Cutting the cord when he was born, I knew some blood would be present but my desire to bring him into this world was greater than my fear of blood. So perhaps my breakthrough and even yours is finding something bigger than our fear. When our motivation and "Why" becomes greater than our will, then we may well find enough strength to muster the ability to overcome. Noted, while I am not a fan of blood in general the biggest reaction is when it is my own. I often think about the stories we tell ourselves, sometimes we have to change our frame of mind.

If I can talk myself around, realise what's going on and why, perhaps I can control or minimise the fear in some way. It sometimes works though isn't easy to master. The last time I had a blood test I decided to reframe my mind and the way

I was thinking. Firstly, I decided that doctors are there to help me, they don't want to hurt me, secondly the reason I was having a blood test was to check that I am okay, again that's reasonable and it's great we have a health care system which is able to monitor and observe if there are issues which need to be addressed. Lastly it would take the best part of five minutes and then I can go back to my day as usual. Once we start to change our story and the narrative we tell ourselves surrounding the fear we face, we can then start to tap into our own power and start to overcome.

As a man we have a huge responsibility to be brave and strong, to not show weakness. Men we need to be honest with ourselves and lay down our own egos. Whether you acknowledge it or you deny it, if you're fearful you are fearful and that's okay. They say courage is feeling the fear and doing it anyway.

One of my biggest fears is "Do I Matter." I love to contribute and I love to feel a part of something bigger than myself. I love the opportunity to give of myself. I love when others ask me for help. I get a kick out of helping others. The emotional complexities of wanting to matter run deep through me. This fear doesn't always work out for me, perhaps at times I present myself as intense and overcompensate wanting to connect or involve myself in some way with another. It may not actually appeal to others, I may come across as needy or attention seeking and I am sure by my own admission that would be an accurate evaluation, however it's not all bad. I want to mean something to you, I do give a rip. I will give my all to my fellow man or fellow woman if they respect and appreciate my time and energy. Wanting to matter is because I feel I was created to make others feel good, to make others understand, make others be more compassionate, kind and gentle. I can't express that if I can't have fellowship with other human beings. I want to receive what I want to give. Not everyone is capable or framed that way. Get real about your fears, where they hide and examine what they prevent you from doing. Some fears for me don't need to be faced, they can be reduced by you not giving them an opportunity to breathe. A good example would be rollercoasters. I am not a big fan of them, do I really have to overcome that fear? I don't think I do, it adds nothing extra to my life if I do or don't go on one. It's not costing me. Some fears do cost us, these are the ones we need to address. For example, a fear of flying prevents people from traveling and seeing the world and tasting of its diversity and culture. It reduces certain opportunities if we allow this fear to control our ability to fly. A fear like this is exactly a fear you need to wage war on.

I think it's worth reiterating that there are two main fears which we are faced with, those that are rational and those that are irrational, while there are some differences to how we approach the differing fears there is also grounds for a change of tactic when faced with such fears.

Irrational fears must be faced with logic, look at the facts, facts can help reduce the severity or likelihood of the threat. Start telling yourself a different story, rather than saying "I may get sick." Start thinking more like "I am healthy." We tend to have more healthy days than sick days in our lifetime, if that's not the case for you, I am truly sorry. We need to take back our own confidence and belief that things will work out for our greater good. I expect good things to happen to me not the opposite. Our irrational thoughts lead us to the fear of something which actually has no direct threat to us at any given moment, often speculative. Speculation is the enemy of peace, it's a projection but there is no direct link of immediate harm to you in anyway.

If the fear is rational then a different approach is often necessary. Some fear can keep us away from danger, knowing the risk and then eliminating that risk is wisdom and sensible. Rational fear is something we are mindful and conscious about. It enables us to protect ourselves from unnecessary harm and danger. It's important to acknowledge and confront fear, it's important to evaluate it and see if it has any merit which may serve us or at the very least preserve us.

Sometimes it's a helpful exercise to let your mind run away with you for a moment, perhaps consider what is the worst outcome that could take place with the fear you're faced, sometimes looking at the worst of something can change the way you look at it and indeed reduce its power and grip over you, ask the trusted question "will this kill me?" If the answer is no, then perhaps that's just the comfort you need to not allow the fear to control you and keep moving forward.

We can master fear if we confront it, if we acknowledge it and assess its validity and then make wise choices to either dismiss or position ourselves and our thinking in a way which will produce peace and strength. You can set a timer for how long you are willing to worry about something. Sometimes I set a ten-minute timer and allow whatever negative emotions I am feeling to have their place, once the timer goes off, I draw a line under it and move on. Dealing with fear is always best served with action. Don't allow it to bully you, but also don't ignore it. You need to explore why, are the issues something internal or external, if you look at the fear it may well open up a huge opportunity for you to grow as a human.

Keep considering, do you need to solve this fear, or can you move away from it, the fear is still there but it's no longer being entertained by you and your imagination. If we are smart and brave enough we can actually allow fear to influence us into good choices and decisions but we have to make sure our relationship with it is held in the right way. Fear is not something to fear but something to consider and then adjust.

How to deal with fear:

- Very few decisions made out of fear are good ones
- Try to be logical
- Don't base fear and choices on ifs and buts
- The way to deal with fear is with action
- When I am afraid I have to shift my energy, exercise helps, go for a run
- Know that fear will pass, it always does

Chapter 7 - Anxiety

Oomph, I would say I have not felt so much anxiety then over the past twenty-four months. It almost seems that the older we become, the more anxiety we are susceptible too. We obviously collect knowledge and experience as we go through life but somehow we lose that childhood bravery because now our head gets in the way and stops us from exploration or taking risks because of "What May Happen" but what may and what will happen are very different.

It may seem simple what I am about to reveal but for me it's another important revelation in order for me to better deal with my anxiety. It could also help you face yours. The simple crux of the matter is that I feel anxiety most when I lose control of a situation. I have flown so many times and while I have experienced a few dodgy flights we have always landed safely and yet even to this day, when I fly I don't fully relax and find true peace. On reflection it's because I am really putting my life into the hands of a pilot that I don't know from Adam. Seems a little dramatic I know, but the reality is I don't know how to fly, so if something goes wrong to the plane or the pilot I am at risk. Anxiety for me isn't a 24/7 problem, but it does rear its head on occasion and when it does we have the same two responses, fight or flight. Both responses don't always serve us best. Anxiety is found between what I can control and what I can't. Three months and counting of lockdown in the UK due to covid is something that pricks my anxiety. I would not choose these past three months, so many restrictions, so many things that feel and operate differently and so many things which were once there are now not. I can't control any of it, the government is doing that and as a law-abiding citizens I comply.

Anxiety lives in the area I have no control of, it lives in relationships, it lives in situations where I cannot affect it. So we have to accept things we did not choose for ourselves and that is something which takes a lifetime to get a hold of.

As a man it's hard to confess you feel anxious, we are not supposed to feel it, we are men, we are supposed to be bullet proof. It's all lies, before we are a man we are a human being. We are all the same regardless of the sex, we all have emotions, we all have a soul, a spirit and a mind. We are all susceptible to the challenges of life, some of us have a different experience due to our upbringing, our culture and our past.

I am thankful that I don't have a lifestyle of anxiety, I am not a worrier. I get little strands of it which manifest in my life depending on triggers. Relationally I like to know I matter, I like to know that even when we are not talking I am still at the front of your mind. I sometimes do get anxious that those I love, love me back and regardless of what happens in life that love will always be there, but my experiences have sometimes been different and one thing we cannot do is control another person, outside of family we can't control the will or emotions of another, we have to accept what they do or don't give. It's not easy is it?

My environment is something I have always been sensitive to, I know the three-month lockdown in my apartment has been tough, I have a fabulous apartment, I am blessed and thankful for it, but not having the choice to leave it and go do something that I enjoy or partake in a distraction is really quite difficult.

So how do I cope with anxiety?

- Talk it through with someone else
- Practice breathing exercises
- Watch the narrative you keep telling yourself
- Pray or meditate
- Remind yourself to focus on the things you can't control
- Accept things for the way they are even if you don't like it or choose it for yourself
- Engage the sensors, for example go smell a candle which makes you feel warm or relaxed.

Anxiety always breeds in the future, if you are able to focus on this very moment and realise that your reality is a safe one right at this very second, anxiety never lives there. It is when we start to focus on something in the future, it's always based on what is ahead, what could or may happen is not the same as what will happen. We must do more to ground ourselves and ignore the temptation to speculate about the future and in doing so stir up fear, worry and anxiety,

When it comes to anxiety or any problem the first thing we must all do is get very clear on what the problem actually is, until we know what the problem is we can't find a strategy to tackle it or take it on, we have to drill deep into the problem and really define it. After we have defined it we must then ask ourselves "What can I do and what can't I do?" to shift, change or alter this current form of anxiety. You then can ask yourself "What do I know and what don't I know?" with regards to the subject matter. Very simple questions, but very important in helping each of us move through anxiety which we all face at some point or another.

Sometimes the anxiety we face is found in our relationship with others, we simply can't control other people, so we must accept the way things are and the way others are and then work hard accepting the premise of where things are right now. Focus your actions and energies which take you away from the past and away from the future and firmly cement you in this very current moment of NOW. Right now is where you find your peace, anxiety is found in tomorrow, it's found in the next minute but it's never found in the right now.

One of the types of therapy psychologist use is called "Compassion Therapy" it's simply looking upon yourself and others with high levels of compassion and empathy. It's really about meeting with yourself whatever state you're in and accepting who you are or accepting how someone else is. I have found it most useful that when I have done something not so smart to meet myself with as much grace and forgiveness as I do with disappointment. At times I have even spoken to the little Mark as a child. Just recently my sister sent me a picture of herself and me. I was perhaps five-years-old and my sister eight-years-old. When I looked at this picture of a five-year-old me, I actually had very warm and positive thoughts and feeling towards myself, I looked like a very lovely, happy and cheeky boy, it was nice to see. I know my childhood had moments of challenge and extreme sorrow and sometimes when I reflect on those moments I actually imagine and picture myself and I speak to the little me and I offer myself compassion and grace and speak healing to myself. A very simple thing to do but if my anxiety is found in something which stems from my childhood as often many of our anxieties do, it's very important to be able to address and help soothe any moments of pain from the past by now dealing with them in the present.

If you can't control how others are... then work on accepting the premise of the here and now. Do things that put you in the here and now.

Chapter 8 - Doing What's Right

There is a saying that goes something like this "Do what is right, not what is easy." Whenever I think upon this it makes me think of integrity and attitude. Having the courage and strength of character to make the right choice has to be grounded in it being ethical. Every day we have small and big choices which are presented in front of us, often our choices are swayed by our own moral compass and values.

I have often said anything of value will cost you something. Often the path which is less travelled is normally the right one for you and me to take. There are always consequences for the choices we make. We live in a world where this way of thinking is becoming more and more tested. We live in a world of pleasure, we live in a world of quick fix and we live in a world where we no longer want to be inconvenienced. We are starting to be conditioned in the choices we make and we have become lazy and unethical in our choices because we want the easy way out.

When I went through my divorce it was important that I was fair in separating assets and managing the delicate intricacies in a way that still honoured my ex-wife, after all she is the mother of my children and doing right by her really equates to doing right by my children. Divorce is painful for many reasons and it's easy to then just think about yourself, I had choices, I made decisions but throughout the process I was mindful and fair.

Sometimes doing the right thing is less rewarding, sometimes we need to do the right thing even if there is no reward, no thank you, no gratitude. It says something about your character. I heard it said that integrity is really having the will and action despite an audience, so doing the same thing regardless if you have someone watching you or not.

I have to be able to sleep at night, my conscious is elevated to a high viewpoint, I can't stand having a conflict within myself and the problem in the conflict is me. I have at times had to change my choice and/or decision because it was not sitting right with me. It takes humility to apologise and to change your mind, but change your mind you should if you know deep down in your heart it's the right thing to do.

As men we must lead by example, we must not be tempted to be greedy, controlling or take advantage of a person or situation, we must make choices with honour and character. We have a responsibility to ourselves and our families to live out of a higher standard of living.

Doing what's right will always feel like a test, if you make a decision and it doesn't feel right you can always change it or take responsibility for it, but it's best to be clear with your convictions and choices before you act. I am sure you each have an example of when perhaps you found some money in a purse or handbag and you handed it into the police, in doing so you then are given a reward as a kind gesture for doing the right thing, but even if there is no reward, you've done the right thing, as one day you may lose or misplace something and you would hope that karma would mean you would get it back too.

When you do the right thing you prove you are trustworthy and honourable, sometimes that can come back to you in the most interesting of ways. I have known companies to test peoples integrity during a job interview, I have witnessed firsthand when a scenario was put to someone and they asked if they would be willing to go along with it if there was some financial reward for them doing so, they said no it's not ethical, at the end they commended the individual for their integrity and was one of the reasons they were hired.

It's vitally important to keep leading by example, that's not just for the benefit of those around you but it's for the benefit of you, you and I have to lead ourselves by example, we need to create a highly focused standard to the way we live and the way we act, it's not about putting unnecessary pressure on ourselves but it is about intentional living and showing our children and our world what living a good life really looks like, the world more than ever needs men and women to stand up and lead by example, the only way to lead by example is through strong and solid actions of kindness. There is always a reward for good actions. If you follow your moral and value compass and you act out of these 2 places the very least you can expect is a warm feeling inside for a job well done. When you follow your values and you don't compromise on your ethics it will quickly promote the inner peace we all need in order to find some purpose and tranquility within ourselves even when the world around us is going bonkers.

Inner peace will ignite the fire of self-belief, when you keep showing up, when you live out of your true self, life will start to make much more sense and your hunger for it will continue to scale new heights. As you continue to reward yourself for doing what is right you actually increase your self-understanding and reduce the relationship you ever had with the unsettled feelings we each have faced when we've taken the easy way out or when we haven't lived out of our true core. Never ever compromise your sense of self, follow your sense of self be fully conscious and engaged with each decision you make, it will serve you and protect you.

We must all refrain from the temptation of quick fixes to problems, very rarely do they turn out to your favour, stick to your core principles, those principles make you who you are. Who you are is found in what's important to you and what do you really want to be and who do you really want to be known by and for? Remind yourself of your inner truths, my children will learn much more from what I do and not just from what I say. Do your actions back up your words? It's easy to say I love you than it ever is to show it.

Compromising yourself, not honouring your inner truths is a form of self-harm and it must stop, reflect on those moments where you went against your core, it will be painful to admit but the truth is, if you don't go against your core value you won't end up landing on your own sword and you won't be broken, the quickest way to break a man's spirit is for that man to betray himself and go against his own truth.

Doing the right thing has its benefits and rewards

- Improves and maintains your reputation
- Promotes harmony for yourself and others
- Makes you trustworthy
- It's more likely that someone else will do you right if you do them right
- We all reap what we sow (Karma)

Chapter 9 - Being the Bigger Man

As men we have a big opportunity to take our place in society and lead the way but sadly we sometimes abuse our position and our power against other men and indeed against women. It often takes a lot, to be the bigger man in situations and relationships.

I can think of two early memories in my working career where being the bigger man wasn't easy or comfortable and on both occasions there was a fight and wrestle within me. I will go ahead and share them the best I can.

The first was when I worked in one of the UK's finest castles. I had received an email from a colleague in a different department to mine, I won't go into all the details but it was one of those emails which when you read it, it leaves you feeling more than a little miffed by the contents. So much within me wanted to fire an email back and felt vindicated and justified to make sure the recipient received the same level of annoyance as I did. Before I did this, I did pause. Which isn't easy to do when you have anger pent up inside you, but it certainly pays to hold yourself in a moment even if it isn't easy and you can see yourself playing out your own version of Gollum in your head.

I decided rather than shooting an email back in anger, I would be the bigger man and go over to his department knock on the door of his office and have it out with him there. The very fact I turned up at his office made him squirm in his chair, I politely said "I would like to talk to you about this email you sent me." I had it out with him and encouraged him in future to be a man and look me in the eyes and discuss any issues he had with me to my face. Many of us don't like conflict and in some cases it is wise to not go face to face with another man depending on the subject, sadly some men see the confrontation of another as a chance to be aggressive and dominant. I didn't want a fight, I wanted resolve. If I had sent an email back, the problem would have escalated and too often the written word can be misunderstood. So take it from me, face-to-face communication is the best way to solve the majority of issues even if it is uncomfortable.

The second story which springs to mind was back in the days I worked in hospitality. If you have ever worked in the industry you will realise it's one of the most thankless and humbling jobs you can do, sadly a small minority talk to you like a third-rate citizen and show as much respect to you as they do to shit on the bottom of your shoe.

I was serving one family, I always offered attentive and high energy service, I took pride in all I did. This particular family were what I call "needy." Of course, when you're in the industry your main responsibility is to enhance the experience and create a theatre ambience where guests feel welcomed and looked after, but this family thought the only people in the restaurant was them, they ran me ragged and showed little compassion and understanding for the duties I was trying to perform not only to them but to my other guests. The upshot of this story is they felt I wasn't available to them at each bark and call and made a complaint to my manager.

My manager called me into the office and explained the situation, he knows the level of service I give and yet he asked something of me which I found difficult. He said to me "Mark, I know you've not done anything wrong here, but I want you to apologise to the family." "Oh my goodness, even now I think I wanted to slap them let alone apologise.

I did somehow find a way to apologise and be the bigger man. At the end of the shift my manager thanked me and he said he knew he was asking a lot of me but knew I had it within me, the family left happy.

Being a bigger man is not easy when typically some offence maybe involved, after being bigger is keeping your mouth shut, walking away, not reacting out of hurt or anger. It's about not responding to someone's provocation. It's also about moral dilemma, it's about doing the right thing. It's about forgiveness, grace and understanding. It's about doing someone right even when they do you wrong. Being bigger is about doing the opposite of what could be a justifiable way to respond.

I think there are right moments to respond but the opportunity lays more within how you respond. I don't believe men should ever be passive, we shouldn't accept or witness poor and bad behaviour or attitude from others. We can all be triggered in some way or another. We get angry when we find the behaviour of others to be insulting or unfair, we must do all we can to pause before we respond but I can't say it's not always a bad thing for people to see anger or even express it, there is a difference between anger and aggression. If we take Jesus, a man without sin, he was angry and furious when people had turned the church into a market stall and he turned tables in anger, it was not reverent or befitting for

70

something so sacred to have something so every day take place.

It's worth noting that a position we may hold doesn't mean we are always right, If I, a father to my children, I don't always do and say the right thing by them, that's why it's important to apologise and be the bigger man, it's also true in the workplace, the boss isn't always right, the position you hold doesn't make you right, it gives you a great responsibility to carefully decide how you lead and treat people.

Not many of us take up the mantle of being the bigger man, there is a great opportunity for us to step into that role and see the positive consequences of those actions.

How to be the bigger man:

- Take responsibility and initiate in putting things right or into motion
- Forgive but don't forget
- Know when to walk away, walking away is not a sign of weakness but strength
- Don't react or retaliate or seek revenge, learn to let go
- Stay true to your core values and don't get sucked into negative drama

Chapter 10 - Starting Over

Starting over is not always easy, often people don't get started on a project because the size of the project just buries them before they've even taken the first step. If we take writing a book for example it's crazy how many people talk themselves out of doing it purely because they pick up a book, hold it in their hand, flick through the pages and think "I hardly get six hours of sleep a night, how can I find the time to write?" You've given yourself an objection and it is no longer contested.

I have a great ability at helping clients actually break down to small daily habits a series of actions, behaviours and exercises that if compounded over time they will achieve that which they want. Let me run with the idea of writing a book, it's a great way to express what I am getting at here. I often ask people "what is a book made up of?", they answer pages, I then ask, "what is a page made out?" of and they say words. Beautiful. So now I say to them if we focus not on the book and not even on the pages but on the words, is that manageable? If I say to you to write a thousand words each day, after 50 days you could have your 50,000 word count which translates into a book, there you have it, wallah!

We become so engrossed on building the house, we become so burdened and defeated by the size of the project, task at hand or even the life we really want that we become discouraged and talk ourselves out of it as quickly as the idea came to mind. It's bonkers! We must rather than focus on the size of the house we are wanting to build we need to focus on laying a few bricks, laying bricks every day over time will start to formalise the main structure of the house. Rome wasn't built in a day, it takes time.

If you use this way of thinking and shift the focus from the end result to a daily action that will take you there, now you are setting yourself up for achievement.

I honestly believe it's the same for relationships. Going through a divorce after being with a partner for five, ten and in my case fifteen years isn't easy to then just start over. It takes time to heal, shift, reflect, breathe and assess. When you do decide to date again, I believe only you can decide that, everyone talks about taking a long period of time to go back into a relationship and while there may be some wisdom in that, life doesn't always work that way and who says it has to, it's your life, so you must decide.

I love to reframe one of the habits from Steven Covey's books "7 Habits of Highly Effective People". My favourite habit is this "start with the end in mind." It's so important when starting over whatever it is, that you have the end in sight. If you decide you want to get married in the future it is stupid being with someone whom you have no intention of marrying. I tend to live my life like this, I start with the end in mind. It will save you a lot of heartache and time too if you can grasp the same principle.

With relationships we often decide what we want in a partner and for most people that may look ambitious, but let me encourage you, it's good to have standards when it comes to relationships, when you know your worth you know what is acceptable within your value system and what is a deal breaker before you end up falling in love with the wrong person. Where most people fall down in relationships and where I feel the greatest opportunity is and most specifically for men, we identify the kind of woman we want to be with but we don't reflect and take time to consider what kind of man do I need to be in order to attract such a woman. This is why self-development and constant reflection of your own development is so so crucial. There is nothing more attractive to a woman than a man who has intelligence.

Starting over in life when you've been through something like a divorce takes times and it takes courage. In some ways it feels like you're going back to school, the great thing is, you have way more knowledge and experience than before, they say that the same lesson will keep repeating itself in your life until you've learned the lesson. Sometimes when things go wrong, you're actually in a healthier position in the present and future because you've just found out what doesn't work, this can encourage you to take heart and move forward.

Things to consider when starting over:

- What is most important to me (Start with the end in mind)
- What is it I really want from life?
- What is it that I really don't want from life?
- What do I want my life to look like?
- Who do I need to be in order to attract the right people and opportunities into my life?
- What is actually the most important?

- What are my core values and how do I need to safeguard them when I make my future decisions?

Chapter 11 - Admitting It's Over

I am not into quitting much, so when you are left with the option of walking away, admitting it's over, it's not something that I take lightly or indeed something that comes quickly in my thought process. To walk away from something is not overly in my nature, I like to stick things out, see if I can find a way, I love to problem solve. On the contrary I would say large parts of society tend to give up at the drop of a hat, as soon as something becomes painful, difficult and uneasy people often tend to trade in their problem or inconvenience for something more appealing and less stressful.

For me the most courageous act for a human being to admit to is knowing when something has come to its end. It is bitter-sweet. Bitter for the pure fact there is a sense of failure attached to the decision and sweet in the sense you are liberated by your own admission that you can't do it anymore. Knowing when to walk away from a job is pretty different from walking away from a relationship.

While I do not want to go into great personal details with regards to my own marriage out of respect and protection of others. Of course I had reached a point in my thinking and assessment when I decided my marriage was indeed over. The sensation of accepting that my marriage had reached the end of the road wasn't easy to accept or easy to admit. Regardless of all the ins and outs, the failings and the mistakes. A relationship takes two people to make it work and two people to make it fail. Some people don't like the word fail or failure, but sometimes you can't gloss over reality, my marriage did fail and it failed because two people failed to make it work, while we both received professional and Christian help during our difficulties we were unable to solve them. I made the decision that our marriage reached the end of the road.

When children are involved it's the hardest and most challenging decision of all. They don't deserve it. They never chose it and they were certainly not responsible. I am proud of the way my ex-wife and myself for the most part have dealt with the pain and complexities of limiting the pain that maybe inflicted on our children in the way we continue to love, support, reassure and validate them and protect them from any sense of being responsible or sharing any of the blame. It's so important that the children know we are still family, just that what that family looks like, looks different now.

It took me many many years to find the faint peace that I could make this decision and admit it's over. I needed to be able to look my kids in the eye and honestly tell them I tried my best to make things work but it wasn't enough, I wasn't able to find a way through. It's a humbling experience, not one that was made over night but a gradual acceptance. Sometimes accepting is the door to the exit and eventually freedom.

All my life I have fought and wrestled and hoped and prayed for change. I rarely think of accepting situations the way they are as a first port of call. I don't like to give up, I don't like to accept when the cards are not the cards I want.

People say play the cards that are in your hand. I have come to know if I don't like my cards, I can get a new deck. I must stress all relationships have challenges, stress and arguments. That's normal. I am not advocating to walk away or quit at the first sign of a problem, you have to evolve, do the work, apologise, seek help, focus on improving yourself, but if you have done those things and you're still not happy, fulfilled and experiencing love over an extended period of time then maybe accepting it's at the end of the road is the only way out.

It's a very delicate and personal choice, I have to reiterate that all of our choices in life tend to have consequences. While admitting something is done is liberating, there is also huge fall out from making the decision to walk away regardless of what it is.

Like with all things you must do what you believe is right for you and that includes being mindful of those you love and care about, you should not sacrifice your own wish for someone else but you should take it into account. Courage is what is needed in order to make such a decision, just like the lion in the wizard of Oz, he had the ability to be courageous he just didn't know it or believe it. You can't hide your inner truth, if you do you will become frustrated and unable to find true happiness and fulfilment. So you must find courage, the belief that things will work out, that people will heal and you will laugh and smile again. I had to be courageous, and finally I am seeing pockets of the life and happiness I believed I could have.

If we focus on courage we only have to look back on the times in our life when we didn't think we could do something and then we did it, we surprised ourselves, we shocked ourselves. In some ways we talk ourselves out of many things by the what ifs, possibilities and maybes, unless things are certain you always have a choice, we sometimes have to fight for what we want. Courage doesn't always come overnight, they say courage is really feeling the fear and doing it anyway. Regardless of what choices you make, never hide your inner truth, never deny what you believe, go after it even if others are not so enthusiastic as you.

The biggest challenge at the moment in marriages and the biggest moral dilemma is the pain and upheaval divorce can have. I understand all of the risks and the pain, I am mentioning this next point because I believe it's crucial and is the one choice which is the most tempting but actually will trump the devastation of a divorce, something that will eventually cause you and your ex-partner harm and even increase the risk of harm to your children in the future. You may be wondering what it is and it's simple. Don't stay in your marriage playing happy families when secretly you are having an affair with someone else. Don't keep living like that, walk away while you can still have some pride. Either be faithful and work through your challenges or walk away and be honourable. The temptation is to play happy families and secretly have a second life. It doesn't work, it causes more pain and will take longer to heal. It's hard but don't stay and emotionally leave or check out, if you do that you're just prolonging yours and everyone else's imminent suffering. Be courageous about how you feel and where you're at, be courageous with yourself and those around you.

When it maybe the right time to accept its over?

- When your heart is no longer in it

- That despite your best efforts no resolve has been found
- When it no longer functions or serves you
- When it doesn't make you happy
- When you keep getting hurt
- When there is no real possibility of reconciliation

Chapter 12 - Looking into your Children's Eyes

I always think before you pull the trigger and end a marriage especially with children involved you need to be able to look in their eyes and be sure and confident you did all that you could to make things better, work through the problems and at least get some sort of professional help before you make such a painful and consequential decision or ending something you had no intention of doing when you took your vows.

It takes courage and a thorough examination of your heart to know you've done as much as possible and accept it isn't enough. I think it's important to me to be able to walk openly and honestly before my children and also my God. I feel a great responsibility to protect, guide and watch over my children even more so since me and their mom separated.

It is the biggest pain and sorrow I feel because no child deserves to experience a one-dimensional family unit. I am sorry for their sakes for the situation which developed and the challenges they have all faced and yet I am so proud and amazed at their resilience and courage despite their understandable pain and needing time to adjust to a new normal they have reached a level which is comforting and gives me some reassurance to the fallout of a broken marriage and in this case a broken family, how our family looks now is very much different to how it used to be. It's so important your children and mine know we are still family it just looks different.

I echo my sentiments which I have shared in past literacies where I mention that I do not want to be the greatest mentor possible if it means I can't be the best father to my children that's humanly possible. Sometimes I think I am a great dad and other times not so much, the one thing I love about children and in particular mine, is their ability to forgive quickly, to move on from hurt, they don't let it fester, they are such a joy. As adults we should feel ashamed of the way we respond to some incidences and take a leaf out of a child's book.

Even if I do something wrong, perhaps I get angry at them for something they did, but it's more about me and my attitude rather than their behaviour. Five minutes later they love me just as much, hug me and kiss me and tell me they love me. Yet some adults I know still hold onto offence which happened many years ago and with no malice intended continue to treat me differently.

I don't understand the coldness and judgement of people, they look at the speck in my eye and don't see their huge blank of wood in their own eye. I love children for the very reason I shared and as men we owe it to them to be much better role models than we've ever been.

I have always loved being a present and loving father. I love it, I find it the most natural relationship. It's not work for me, it's a pure joy. As men and for those of us who are fathers, it is vitally important that when we get it wrong with our children we are humble enough to go back to the child and say sorry and own when we get it wrong. I have always tried to practice that because I believe it teaches children to forgive but also own their mistakes.

We all make mistakes, we all get things wrong but when I look into my kid's eyes, I want to see happiness, confidence, peace and love. I want to be able to look them in the eye and be truthful and be real. We need more humanity between parents and their children, between a father and his sons and daughters. If the world is not getting better it's because as parents we are not living a life which is a good example of the children we want to raise. Attitude always reflects leadership.

It's not an easy path, it takes a long time to process all that has taken place but it will serve you to remember why you left, why you made that choice to go your separate ways. We have to learn to stand strong in our decisions, back yourself. It's all about the base (Yes, that does make me want to break into a song and dance!). But when you look at it, all our choices and decisions should be based on our core values and what it is we really believe in, thankfully such a big decision doesn't happen every day and the impact a decision normally has isn't normally so complex.

When we make choices which don't deviate from who we really are, what we really believe in and what matters most to us, we will be able to ride out most storms over a period of time. We have to own our own choices and stand true to our "why". Yes everyone will have an opinion about your choices, so let them, but reassure yourself nobody has walked a day in your shoes, nobody experiences everything the way you do, we all have our own private, personal and exclusive understanding and experiences.

We need time and space to start to recreate a new dimension of family life and we can do that by honouring and respecting each family member involved in the painful process of changing how the family looks and feels. That was something which we were so careful about with the children. We reassured them that we were still a family, just that how the family looked would change. We all know children learn by what they see, way more than what they will hear.

Children are often at more harm seeing, witnessing and being involved in a loveless relationship between two parents, it's now my goal and challenge to show them what a wholesome relationship really looks like so when they have adult relationships and marry themselves they have a good understand of what that looks like and what a healthy loving relationship really is.

I love being a dad, my children have even joked with me about when they are parents how they believe their own kids will love me more than they will love them because they respect and honour me as a loving kind daddy, I am proud that my kids know I am kind and loving and enjoy my company. Of course I can improve as a dad, of course I make mistakes, occasionally I say or do the wrong thing and I do my best to own that and say I am sorry.

I now need to show them what it's like to be a loving partner to my girlfriend and what it really looks like to be a loving husband, my son needs a role model and my daughters need to see what is acceptable from a man's behaviour and what isn't. Due to the fact me and my ex-wife treat our children with respect it will teach them what is acceptable behaviour from another and what isn't. Hopefully it will protect them from making poor relational choices because they know their own worth and value.

My children are an expression of how they are raised. When they become adults the impressions and examples they have seen from their mother and I will be the catalyst to the way they form relationships and make key decisions for their life. When I look into my kid's eyes I see love and innocence, I want to protect them from the harshness of the world which is created by human interaction. I want to answer them truthful and make decisions and I want to conduct myself in a way that makes them proud, that protects their name and honours them as a good father and a good Godly man.

Things to consider when you know one day your kids may ask you what happened:

- Make sure you've looked for help in the form of counselling or equivalent
- That you are making tough choices with the right intentions
- Understand it may take years before your child may fully understand and accept the way things are
- Don't become too upset if a child or one of your children shows more loyalty to your partner than you

Chapter 13 - Self-Conflict

It's really difficult when we are left with a scenario where we are torn with what to do. It's not so easy when such a conundrum presents itself. A couple of things spring to mind when you are torn over a decision to make. Firstly, never make a major decision in a valley. This means that when you have to make a big call over something which will have substantial consequences never make such a decision in the midst of you being in a low place (Valley). When you make decisions ideally you want to be in a place of clarity, rest and understanding (Mountain).

The second thing that comes to mind is to always sleep on key decisions before you fire the gun, always be mindful of what pressure you're feeling and whether fear is playing a role in influencing you within your imminent choices. It pays to remind yourself of the key message "Do what's right, not what is easy."

Too often we try and make decisions that will hopefully please everyone, it's mere impossible everyone is going to be happy with the choices and key decisions you make. So with that in mind, it's better to make decisions based on your core belief systems and values and navigate from that position when self-conflict arises within you.

It is uncomfortable when it's hard to decide which way to go, it's hard when one option looks more glamorous, simple, easy and the other more unglamorous, complex and the need to work at it. In gambling terms the phrase " is often shared in the context of winning and losing money, when you're gambling it's easy to both win and lose money, you just can't always control which one you will get. Sometimes when things are handed to you on your lap, you don't value the essence of the commodity you hold, but if you had to work at it, sacrifice social time and make regular time commitments to receive the same commodity you would probably value it more because it costs you something. Anything of real value, whether that's materialistic or a relationship it's going to cost you, time, energy, effort, commitment etc.

During my five-year reflection before I actually decided my marriage had met the end of the road I was conflicted for so many reasons. Firstly, I don't take vows lightly, I pride myself in being a man of my word, if I say I am going to do something I like to follow through on my commitment, I don't like to just talk and then never deliver, that's when you start to become flaky and unreliable. I made a commitment before God and man to let death do us part, while I know it's referring to physical death and I am not trying to tiptoe out of my vows but it was a kind of death that led to the ending of the marriage.

Being a Christian was another source of conflict for me. I know God hates divorce, he says it and probably he hates it for all the reasons I experienced and also witnessed others experience (mainly my kids) because there is always fallout and pain and sorrow. I wasn't sure I could do it because I wasn't convinced at the time God would approve and sadly I knew the judgement of Christians would arrive at my door. I love Jesus and I am called to love my brother and sister in Christ, however sadly Christians are the most judgemental people on the planet, that's not the Jesus I know. I experienced more silence than real criticism, we have all experienced the silent treatment. Of course there were some exceptions to this experience. It pains me to say that during my divorce I experienced more love and understanding from those who don't believe in God than those who do. Regardless of me weighing up these options I continued exploring the options within my soul but acknowledging the deep unrest within me.

God does not condone divorce but I also believe divorce is not a sin, it's just sad. The judgement of others and what they think will never define whom you really are, it will only show you who is for you and who isn't. The contemplation and depth of my thoughts was extensive.

I then had to consider the reality of me exposing my precious beautiful children to something I experienced as a child, the pain of divorce and the breakup of a family. It's not easy to think I would be doing this to not just one child but three. I had to reflect on what made that process most unbearable for me when my parents split and whether I could eradicate and or minimise the effects it would have on my children. Thankfully I think my ex-wife and I were able to handle the process as well as possible, considering the circumstances.

The conflict in me was significant. I felt every weight and burden of responsibility and it took years to reach a point where despite these conflicts and struggles I still had to do something as fundamentally I wasn't happy and I couldn't carry on persevering in something my heart was no longer in and my opportunity for something happier remained a possibility.

The pain of divorce had everything to do with abandonment, I have had an ongoing struggle throughout my life with regards to this emotion of being left behind. I came across a great book called "Attachment Theory". If you haven't read it, please do. There are three main attachments, they are secure, avoidant and anxious. When you know what your attachment style is, it will better help you understand your own reactions and how and why we internalise many things the way we do. Most importantly with attachment its established in childhood. Me being mindful of this helps me strive and be aware of creating a healthy attachment style for each of my children, as of today I would say they all have a slightly different attachment style to each other but I am gently reinforcing and reaffirming a secure attachment so they don't have to deal with some of the struggles I have faced even as an adult having a secure attachment but with some anxious attachment threads which haven't served me but have caused me pain and some of that pain could have been avoided but for the issues of me creating my own pain by internalising situation in a way which was not necessary. It's imperative we take the learnings, we do the research and we find all that we can to help in our decision making and what the fallout of our decisions may be.

A part of my process was helped by a decision I made to go and spend some time alone in Cornwall, my Godfather lived there at the time with his wife. I spent just over a week there to take myself out of my environment and in effect meet myself, my Godfather was there should I need him, he never gave me advice, he just asked me questions. I like to chew on the fat and really search the innermost parts of myself before I make life-altering decisions. During that week I prayed, I cried and I reflected. God did meet me in that place, I poured out of my heart and my soul did find some rest, I walked for miles and miles and on one particular day I walked from one coast to another until a wall stopped me from going any further, I actually call that wall my praying wall. I lay my hands on it every time I go to that part of Cornwall and it reminds me of this week-long soul sabbatical where I met myself and met my God.

After that time away in Cornwall I made the decision to go back to my family and give it one last shot, I needed to know I had tried to find a way through regardless of previous pain or disappointment, I stuck at it for three months but by the end of the three months I knew that my marriage had reached the end of the line but I am so thankful that I had that pause, that I took myself away, if I hadn't, maybe I would feel more guilt and shame. I don't really feel guilt or shame, it's been more disappointment for not being able to fix what was broken.

A change of environment, a change of scene, to come away and meet yourself is so so valuable, important and critical before you make a big choice. Honour yourself with some time out, I really poured myself out, I really looked within, I met with myself and I met with God. Whether you believe in God or not, meet with yourself before you make a big decision.

I acknowledge that it really took me the best part of five years to make a concrete decision. I had a genuine fear of missing out. I had become loss averse. The pain and loss can feel much stronger than the gain. I had lots of thoughts as you can probably tell.

The conflicts within are hard to navigate, sometimes you will choose wisely and other times maybe not so wisely, in most circumstances you don't want a conflict and not everything we are faced with feels like we are choosing which is our favourite child, life would be a lot crueler if the choices we made came at such a cost, most of our choices don't have the ramifications and hurt that some of the more meaningful ones tend to have. I guess the good thing is that I am not careless, I am measured, I consider and I weigh and I take my time before making a decision. Truth be told sometimes you will never know what the decision you make will feel like until you actually make it.

When in self conflict consider these thoughts:

- What do you fundamentally want?
- What are the benefits in the choice you're making?
- What are the downfalls of the choice I am making?
- Does my decision align with my key values?
- Is there a cost or implications in the choices I make?
- Is my choice ethical and moral?
- Does my choice make me happy?
- Am I prepared to own my decisions and accept all the consequences which come with it?

Chapter 14 - Reinvention

I am sat in my Godfather's garden in Cornwall, the sun is on my face, I can hear the sound of many many birds. I am being extremely English and drinking tea and I have tasked myself with writing this chapter about "Reinvention." My Godfather is in his workshop securing some new storage units to the walls and has a soft whistle as he goes about his work. My view is picture perfect, gorgeous bright flowers and a freshly cut lawn capture my attention. Cornwall is about four hours south from where I live and yet each time I come here, it very much feels like I enter into a soul sabbatical. My Godfather has made me some fruit toast and I can pause and breathe deep and listen and sense how my soul is feeling, I can pause and be one with my body, feeling the warmth in my heart. I am taking several deep breaths as I am fully present in my current state.

It always amazes me how a change in environment does wonders for both the soul and the mind. I know this to be true, I have experienced it many many times and am amazed by the results. We sometimes over-emphasise the importance of developing and changing ourselves to a more defined version and yet sometimes it's not you that's the problem, it's your environment.

I find reinvention not only comes from a self-improvement but also reassessing the very area you live, work, explore or become exposed to is a deciding factor of being able to reinvent not just yourself but your world. I have experienced so much change over the last few years, creating a new normal takes time, it's not easy when life looks very different to the life you had before.

Once the wounds have healed or at least started to heal, once the dust has settled and some of the practical responsibilities have been taken care of, you can now shift your attention back onto yourself and discover there is a new way to express yourself and a new way to live, your heart must find that courage and confidence to tap into a new way of not just thinking but living.

There is a huge difference between sitting with a problem and wallowing in it. Divorce will ravish your soul, it will leave you feeling cold, isolated and afraid. It's important to experience and feel the contrasts of life, when life is tough it certainly doesn't seem that enjoyable and in most cases we don't have the ability to frame it the way we would if we were not in the middle of the current difficulty, but when we are able to reflect and see that which is laid before us, we can take stock, we can reevaluate the situation and then make positive steps and choices to rebuild our life. We have to have the courage to first look deep within ourselves and take responsibility for the current situation we find ourself in, while doing so is not always easy, we also must liberate ourselves knowing we cannot control another person, we can't control what they feel, think or decide, we can only accept, which is often the hardest and yet liberating discovery of all.

When there is a break down or a severance in a relationship all the obvious pains and challenges which we face are obvious, however it also presents us with an opportunity, an opportunity to form a better relationship with ourselves and with those around us. Reinvention is necessary in order to take the parts of our soul and our unfulfilled dreams and give them new hope and new energy. I must not be judged as a man until I have drawn my last breath. You can't judge any man or woman at the start or the middle of their journey, only at the end of a man's life can you assess the fullness of what your life really meant to others.

It's so important we look at what gives us both fulfilment when reinventing ourselves. It's an opportunity to express ourselves the way in which it feels like second nature. We owe it to ourselves that on the back end of difficulty or a significant life change that we establish a new baseline of living, creating the right environment for yourself will have a huge impact on reinvention.

When I think of all the failed retailers that no longer exist within our world, the majority of them folded due to an inability to reinvent themselves, they didn't move with the times, they didn't meet public demand, they didn't change based on consumer's needs, they played it safe, they became boring and fundamentally they became irrelevant. While I am not comparing a retail shop to a human life, the principles are the same. If we are going to make our life matter, if we are going to make our "mark" on man then we have to be relevant to ourselves but also those around us. We have to develop a nature and personality which helps us influence our fellow man. We also have to be relevant to give purpose to our life and the mission in which we have set before ourselves to obtain the dreams which lay within us.

Reinvention is the action or process through which something is changed so much that it appears to be entirely new. It's a little like a complete makeover, it can be of the same essence but an entirely different expression, it can be the same person but with a different behaviour. It's important not to lose who you are but equally it's as important to change anything in your life which doesn't serve you, which doesn't make you proud or constantly keeps causing you injury.

I noticed a number of behaviours within me which were causing great personal injury, these behaviours derived from beliefs within myself which I thought were true, but each time I associated myself with these untrue beliefs I would injure myself, I would cause myself pain by misinterpreting the situation I was finding myself in. Over the last few months I have been working with a psychologist to help me identify moments which cause me pain and then start to find interventions which prevent me from injuring myself or misunderstanding situations that sometimes I had very little control over.

In many ways my soul has been going through some reinvention, it's very much me that's going through the process and seeing things for what they are, not always easy when the shadows which lurk within us are exposed or confronted, but either way confronted they must be in order to find healing, breakthrough and relief from the torment which causes ourselves a great harm by our own way of thinking, we now must frame our thoughts and our internal beliefs and start believing that which is true based on this new narrative while being diligent to not be consumed by the stories of others which can knock us off course.

Some of my beliefs needed reinvention, some of yours do too. My reinvention is coming through the help of a psychologist. I could see some behaviours and beliefs which have tripped me up time and time again over the years. If I had been able to heal or lead myself out of them I would have a long time ago. I obviously mentor people on self-leadership. So I believe in the process of getting help from others should we not have the tools, capability or knowledge to get the desired result. For me personally working with a psychologist is something that's been invaluable, I have a lifestyle and business of helping others, I enjoy when I am the subject matter because it enables me to not only grow but also have a greater revelation of who I am, so often we are actually the biggest problem we face in our life, but it takes being brave and honest to admit it and then seek out help.

My belief system needed altering. When you have a clearer sense of self you are able to reduce the amount of hurt you experience from the hands of others and also are not as affected by flattery. I am sure somewhere I have read that insult and flattery should be held in the same regard, regardless of criticism or praise, keep being yourself and stay authentic.

How to reinvent yourself:

- Look at what works and what doesn't and make some subtle changes
- Sometimes it's not what you do but how you do it, sometimes reinvention comes in the form of

execution rather than it necessarily being fundamentally different

- Do something drastic, change careers, change location, change the way you look but make sure you're owning the choices you make here
- Seek out problems and go and fix them, the quickest way to reinvent who you are is to go involve yourself in something which needs a solution

Chapter 15 - Keeping Amicable

Considering I had experienced divorce first-hand as a child, to see the fallout of two parents is sometimes difficult to navigate, a careful path to take when you have to consider children in resolving conflict and doing so with the pain of a broken marriage. It's not easy to always keep your peace, to control your feelings and not respond to each other in a harmful and unhelpful way. You don't have to be Sherlock Holmes to know that there is huge amounts of pain and tension in both people when a marriage has ended.

If I am honest I am proud of the way me and my ex-wife did communicate with our children about the situation at hand. We were both very mindful to protect our children from feeling responsible for the breakup, we both reassured them of our love and that didn't change. My ex-wife and I had agreed that we would do our very best to not bad mouth or belittle each other in front of the children, we realised that if we spoke negatively about the other it actually causes the children pain, they love both parents, they value both parents and regardless of the temptation to complain about the other the intention and mindfulness has always been to honour that as best we can, but of course things can and do spill over and sometimes you miss it.

I think overall how we dealt with our marriage affairs and personal challenges we did with as much grace, compassion and understanding whilst acknowledging it's impossible for something so painful and complex to be resolved without some tears, anger and bruising.

The need to keep things amicable is a good goal and standard of living, if not for reasonable communication but for the sake of dear children which are involved. You still very much have huge responsibilities for little lives when you have kids. Being amicable enables you to communicate on difficult or sensitive issues without it then flaring up the past and previous frustrations. You don't want to get to a point where you start operating and relating to each other like a game of chess, you don't want things to become tactical or calculated. You want to reach a point that this is the decision which has been made, but I respect you as my children's mother and as a human being and vice versa.

The key to being amicable is to be honest, be honest with how you feel, be honest about key information which may affect your children or your ex-partner. Do the right thing, take care of your responsibilities, keep your children as the focus. They really are the innocent party in all of this, I honestly believe for me personally it's the challenges we have given our children based on our failed marriage that gives me the heaviest heart of all. Striving to be amicable with their mom is a key component to keeping things as peaceful as possible and aids better communication which can only be good for children.

As parents we have key decisions we need to make, we still need to be able to talk things through, we need to be able to express our concerns and be aligned with how the children are to be raised. We have had differences of opinion and both our parenting styles have some key differences but we both want more than anything, what's best for the children.

I encourage you all to set an agreement between you and your ex-partner, insist on communication regardless of the pain and sometimes the uncomfortable moments you may find yourself in, it's for the sake of your children. Sit down and agree on some unified house rules. This is to ensure more of a consistency for your children regardless of what house they are in, of course there will be differences of style and approach but not too much deviation, the hardest one I have found and still find tricky is bed times. I typically have my children on the weekends so their need for more sleep is not as necessary on a Friday and Saturday night as it is on a school night where they need to be fresh and well rested, do your best with your ex-partner to find a common ground and stick to it so the children have an understanding and expectation which will help them feel grounded in their new way of living.

How to keep amicable:

- Be honest and clear in your communication
- Do what you say you're going to do
- When you make a plan keep to it (e.g. when you're going to see the children)
- Always do what's right and not what is easy
- Be sensitive to what the other one is thinking
- Keep the children front and centre and it will help navigate making a sound decision when the focus is on the children and not on each other

Chapter 16 - Don't Use
Children as Weapons

It's often very easy to use children as a weapon in order to punish, persuade or guilt trip the other partner after a divorce. Whatever happens, PLEASE DON'T USE CHILDREN as pawns while you try and navigate a new way of doing family from two different homes.

Children are and will always be the innocent party. They didn't choose what I chose or what my ex-wife chose, they are innocent little people who don't need any more turmoil or upset than divorce and a broken family brings to them.

It's inevitable that there is and will be great pain in the hearts of men and women when they go through something so gut wrenching, it is true that hurting people hurt people. Regardless of the justification or temptation to use children as a way to inflict more pain or revenge on your ex-partner, it is totally out of the question. The only ones who suffer are your children.

We must not be tempted to withhold or prevent our children reaching mom and dad at any time they want. Children need to know they are not being divorced or separated from their parents, the only severance is between mom and dad and yet if you have children involved you must do all you can for the sake of them to settle your differences or at the very least agree to disagree and find a way to form a respectful bond.

My ex-wife is a good mother and she is affirmed that way from me to our children. I love the fact also that we have raised our children to have a voice and if they feel either of us speak ill of the other we are challenged. I love that about my kids, they speak up for justice and for honour. We have empowered them to express how they feel. This also helps to ensure our kids are not used to cause pain or punishment for past wrongs.

Since it's been a couple of years since we separated, over time you begin to see the children adjust and adapt. It seems to take two years for the children to start to settle and create a new normal, of course every child is different but as mom and dad honour each other despite the break down, it actually has a positive effect on the children's adjustment and healing process too. They need to see that mom and dad can still communicate and organise and continue to love them even when things look different.

I will say from experience that as a man who is not the main carer of his children, it's really difficult to ask for when you can see them. That means the woman really needs to be as graceful as possible to not use the children as the weapon, I think there is more of a temptation for the main caregiver when families divorce to consider using the children as a way to inflict more agony by making it difficult to communicate with the children. I see my kids regularly and we have settled on a rhythm and routine which helps all parties plan and accept the new way of living.

I would say most nights I speak with my children, it's important that emotionally and relationally we give our children exactly what they want, need and ask for. They need to know always that both sets of parents are available 24/7.

It is so vitally important we help our children transition, in the previous chapter I was encouraging an agreement between two sets of parents, keep some non-negotiable house rules, it's important to set out an agenda of what things will look like, be clear with your children as to what they can expect from you and when you set that expectation be sure to meet it. As with all humans but especially in children, their biggest fear is loss. We must do all we can to combat that fear and we can do that with reassurance and clearly helping them see what does access from one parent to another look like.

I always ask my children how they are feeling and to name their feelings, this is a core life lesson that I am teaching them, how do you feel, what is that feeling and then helping them understand why they have this feeling and how they can move out of that feeling in a positive way. The point here is to help them feel secure in the change of family dynamics. Actually take some time to find out what your children want and need, keep them informed, help them be part of the process, help and encourage them to shape the new routines so they feel included and respected. Set a space and a place for them, give them the ability to express themselves, let them pick the way their bedroom looks and feels, let them have their own space. This is something I am continually looking at giving them.

Over time set up debrief dates and times so that your children can check in with you how they feel things are going, what works and what doesn't work, what they would like to do more of or less of, let them feel valued and included, all of these steps will help your children transition and find the security they desperately need at this time.

The dangers in using children as weapons when settling disagreements:

- The children are innocent
- Your children may resent you for it
- They need a positive example, one day they may find themselves in the same situation as you do
- Children are the only ones who get hurt
- It may cause them psychological problems in adult life

Chapter 17 - Dealing with Failure

Oh the not so lovely friend called "Failure" though I suppose it depends on how you look at it. Some internalise failure as something extremely negative and all it does is short circuit your supply of power and creates an inability which prevents us from being able to correct, change and improve in the area one has failed in.

We must deal with failure in a mature and smart way, if we do that, we will find failure is an ingredient when processed to be one of the most poignant prerequisites of success and growth. I shared in Plot Twist that I have learned so many valuable lessons through failure, that actually I am ready to make some more, since failure just shows you how to not do something or how not to behave or act. It actually helps eliminate future failings and problems.

When we have a revelation of doing something which results in a negative notion, we know not to do the same mistakes again, by eliminating past errors we strengthen our opportunity of success, breakthrough and accomplishment.

As men we fail every single day, in what we think, in what we say and in what we do. Failure if you are creating, shifting, evolving or moving something from A to B will result in the occasional misfortune of failure. Though the reality is actually not misfortune it helps you become fortunate to have the ability to get it wrong and then try again.

Let's stop being afraid of failure and take ownership for when we get it wrong. It is so much more liberating to just put up your hands and accept what you did or didn't do, especially if it didn't actually work out the way you had planned. Don't let it bury you. Be mindful that in spite of either criticism or flattery you are not affected in such a way that you lose centering yourself and staying on an even keel.

Most of the time men want to hide their failure, men are extremely proud, competitive and pumped up with ego so the natural ability to even accept failure is something most men struggle with. We not only should own when we fail but embrace it as a teacher because it just shows us how not to do something. That's when failure becomes your ally and strengthens your ability to move forward.

I clearly failed at times in my role as a husband because while two people are responsible for its success and demise, I am one part of that contributing factor. I have reflected on my failed marriage, I continue to do that to help me with my current new relationship that I am happy to be a part of. Yet it's important I understand my responsibility and what I did or didn't do which will have been a contributing factor in its breakdown.

Being honest takes bravery and a slice of maturity. I have been processing for several months now my failings with my psychologist and I have gained both clarity and strength by dealing with those things which have caused me pain and injury.

As men we need to start owning our mistakes, it's only when we get real can we adjust and grow and be the men that both our women and our world need. Failure is no longer something we need to hide or be afraid of, it's something we need to continue to talk about openly with each other. I find it hugely liberating to say "you know what, you're right, I did get it wrong, I did get it wrong." It feels so much more liberating then trying to defend an action that you yourself know isn't defendable. So don't let your ego or your pride be what response you manifest when you're called out. Accept it and move forward.

My failed marriage is probably the one thing which is the hardest for me to accept. If I have a problem I always find a way, but the complexities of where two are responsible you don't always have the freedom or control to influence all areas to bring about a change.

The problem with a failed marriage is it's so public, it can affect entire communities and sadly people like to talk, to have judgements and cast dispersions upon such heartbreaking news. I find reminding myself that my life is not about pleasing others and the sacrifice of pleasing me but more pleasing myself and God and through that energy and oneness with myself I can please others when I am the full expression of who I am I find my freedom and you will too.

I accept that I am part of the reason why my marriage failed, that feels right to own that, to take ownership for my own mistakes, take the learnings and make sure in my new relationship I am growing and not making similar mistakes.

I think it's important to take a few minutes and actually consider what failure is to you. Write down a few words in your own language, capture what it is for you personally. Then write down what you are afraid of. What we are afraid of is combined by fear and as a man one of our biggest fears is not being enough or fearing a loss of value. Failing at times is an active part of being a human.

One of the key dynamics of failure is being able to forgive yourself. That really is the tonic for all ailments of failure. Self-talk in the form of I will start to do better is a good starting place, then follow that up with positive action which reinforces your desire to do better.

Be honest with yourself and learn to separate the two expectations we are all faced with. Firstly ask yourself, "Am I enough in my own eyes?" then ask yourself "Am I enough in the eyes of others?" Just because others have an opinion of you doesn't mean they are right. I find it helpful here to embrace and call on a trusted friend, someone who has clear motives and has your best interests at heart, we all need someone who can give us genuine guidance and honesty even if it's painful to hear, because if we capture the essence of what they are saying it will help us move forward.

How to deal with failure:

- Understand we all experience failure and it's how we deal with it which will make the biggest difference
- Remember failing is really telling you and others you're trying. He who never made a mistake never made anything.
- Forgive yourself and take the learnings
- Realise if you can digest failure it will serve you and help you find solutions to other problems quickly without you wasting time on tears
- Give yourself a period of time like thirty minutes to wallow in your disappointment and then snap out of

it, sometimes I set a timer and once that goes off I have to shift my energy and refocus my mental frame

Chapter 18 - Judgement of Others

Seems whenever you do something significant, life changing, life altering, controversial and what appears sudden to others you sadly are faced with judgement, accusation, assumption and a shift in the way people relate to you or in most cases when they stop communicating and caring at all.

The one thing I dislike about the Church and from some Christian quarters is the judgement people cast onto others. When I went through my divorce the response was split, a select few checked in, reached out, cared for and loved me through my pain, the majority however said nothing, they remained quiet, no communication, no care. Interesting to experience and yet it's no wonder revival hasn't happened, because sadly the Church often does not look like the head of it, Jesus himself.

It's sad to admit but those who were the most supportive were those who don't even believe in God, those that have never acknowledged him and yet when it came to my support network the vast majority was from those who had no God relationship and yet didn't judge, but comforted, reassured and helped me through.

Judgement sucks. He whom is without sin, cast the first stone. You judge me on my speck in my eye and you have a huge plank in yours. People make judgement calls from the outside in, they have never walked a day in my shoes, they haven't walked a day in your shoes either. Yes, those who I expected to show love or at the very least compassion didn't. I am not bitter or angry, it's just sad that we are treated differently by others who quickly forget their own trouble and challenges.

The reality is I don't need the approval or blessing of any man. I need to remain truthful to myself and walk openly and honestly before God. When you're going through a divorce the last thing you want is people casting dispersions, gossiping and assuming what's happening and how could you leave behind a wife and children. I never left my children, they are my world, my everything. I invest and fight hard to make time and invest in them, I am thankful that as of now I have a beautiful relationship with all my kids and they are a priority to me and what I am seeking to build.

It's never nice to be judged. It shows a degree of arrogance on the one who passes the judgement, judgement does not belong to man. I would like to think that when others have gone through a divorce they have not felt my judgement but my desire to help, comfort and be whatever they may need me to be.

Let me be clear, a couple of very dear friends that love Jesus with all their heart, have loved me through those dark days without judgement, they have been Jesus to me and they know who they are, but my overall reflection during this season in my life is very few people were available, present and willing to hold space when I really needed them to be. As a man I guess we are told to suck It up, either way it doesn't make it easy or enjoyable.

We must live a life true to our own values and beliefs, may we judge ourselves, adapt and change if need be, take responsibility and even apologise, but forget trying to please others. I realised I am my own man, other men around me I don't even want to be like, so why should I try to appease them and do right in their eyes.

When we are judged it's often to make that person feel better about themselves, looking at others disfavourably is a way for others to comfort themselves and acts as a deflection to their own mess and situation. It shows me that they don't love themselves particularly well. If you can't show love and compassion to others it's a good sign you don't show it to yourself. That's not the type of man I want to be.

You don't have to agree with my choices, I am not asking you to, but you don't have to change the way you see me or act towards me because you've decided to play judge and jury without context, facts, insight and walking through the footsteps I have had to take in my life.

We will all face judgements as men. Do we say or do the right thing, do we make the right choices each and every time? The key here is to be able to look yourself in the mirror and own your own shit. It always comes down to being true to yourself, owning your choices and going after what you want in life, if you stay true to you, your moral compass, your beliefs and values, it really doesn't give a rat's ass as to what others think.

It's worth noting that not all judgement is about you and I. I have known in my own life people who have condemned me out of their own fear, they are afraid to rock their own world by impressing the truth I have come to know, I have at times done something which they would love to do but they

112

dare not or feel they can't do it, and then they end up resenting me for it. This is often why people judge because secretly they wish they could take the actions I have but are afraid to do so for whatever reason.

Gossip sadly will always happen but it's down to you and I to decide how it lands within our hearts and spirits. I recently wrote a letter to myself about an uncomfortable situation I found myself in, the letter to myself acknowledges and addressed my feelings and my failings but I also met myself with grace, understanding and compassion. This is a great way to self-comfort and heal. If you find yourself in a difficult situation where you feel you had the right intention but the wrong execution now is a good time to write yourself a letter.

How to deal with the judgment of others:

- Remind yourself not everyone will agree with your choices or decisions and that's okay
- Understand your life is not to please them but yourself and God or your equivalent
- Ignore them, when one points the finger three others point it back
- Simply tell them "He whom is without sin cast the first stone"
- Rise above the criticism stay true to yourself and be comfortable in your own skin
- Accept that it's a part of life

Chapter 19 - Do the Basics

It's amazing when hell is breaking loose how quickly we react and respond to the things in not always the smartest or most helpful of ways and typically when life is challenging, it certainly pays to at least have a number of basics during a struggle or crisis, to stay faithful with. Doing the basics during difficulty can give you a sense of control and meaningfulness while you deal with the aftermath of something difficult like a divorce. Sadly too many people will go towards something like alcohol to try and shift their focus and ease the pain of their current struggle, but in all honesty that will only add to your problems and compound the misery regardless of the short-term relief it may well present itself.

When I talk about basics I am really referring to eating well, sleeping well and exercising. Something for the body, mind and soul is crucial when working out the more intricate and complex situations we find ourselves in. There is a very popular YouTube video about a commanding officer from the Navy Seals and he talks profoundly about the importance of making your bed in the morning. It seems so trivial and insignificant but when times are tough it's the small little victories of preparation that actually help bring normality and courage to our hearts which helps us better deal with the more heavier obstacles we have to negotiate.

During the early months of the Covid outbreak my ability to exercise was paramount to keeping me positive, sane and fit. I walked for miles, and I mean miles. I set myself a goal of 50,000 steps during one day of lockdown and I achieved it with well over 57,000 steps. It gave me a sense of accomplishment, a sense of purpose and got me outside of my own head. Exercise is a basic requirement that all men should partake in without excuse, we need it to let out some frustration and steam. Vigorous exercise is renowned for releasing stress hormones and calming your state of mind.

It's always made me smile because regardless of how stressful life has become, I have never really had any issues with my sleep. Much to the annoyance of most as soon as my head hits the pillow I can fall asleep within minutes. I probably get between 6-8 hours of sleep a night, I really need closer to eight hours.

There is an understanding about the body to mind lead. The premise of this ideal is whatever becomes the leader of you the rest will follow. Hence why it's famous that being out in nature is wonderful for your mental health, your body leads you outside and into nature and then your mind is enlightened and there is a shift in the way you feel. If you take care of your body and it takes you towards health, your mind will follow suit. Small steps are never to be frowned upon, small steps give way to long and extensive journeys of discovery and freedom.

If we can discover small but meaningful hacks which will help you keep to the basics it may be the difference between you taking ownership of something or something taking ownership of you. Leaving your gym wear or running shoes by the front door maybe just the little nudge you need. Setting an alarm to give you a ten-minute warning before getting into bed could also be a small but meaningful adjustment.

My Fitbit has been such a motivator this year, keeping me accountable to achieving 10,000 steps daily, sometimes technology can really help us. We must dare to feel and plan our week even if that doesn't come naturally to us, my ability to plan and create a routine is fundamentally what helped me push through the mental fight I had going on in me through the pandemic we all faced. Keeping an overview of your week and creating space for all the things you can control and care about is what then re-empowers you and brings that sense of control, we all need at times to keep anxiety at bay and adopting these strategies will help. None of us want to create stress before activity, we want to be clear on what we are going to focus on and then execute. When we achieve we feel strengthened and more positive.

How to do the basics:

- Be consistent and habitual in your daily actions and routines
- Make them non-negotiable, there is no room for manoeuvre or change
- Prioritise yourself, you can't give out of an empty cup
- Enjoy the basics, they are your bread and butter and foundation to building something more glamorous and successful
- Remind yourself that your basics give you health and ensure you have the energy to live the life you want

Chapter 20 - Disappointment with Others

I think we all battle with this one on a fairly regular basis. Sometimes we have too much of an expectation on our fellow man and we think those around us have the ability of God or we are choosing poorly who to build a relationship with or those who we are in relationship with, really need to step up their game.

During my divorce I had four individuals who I could rely on and who I journeyed with during this time, others who I expected to play a pivotal role went missing or silent. Needless to say, when it comes to relationships if people don't make the time I don't tend to give them much opportunity to hang around. Right or wrong in most cases it serves me well. It's left me with a trusted core few whom I do life with, while honouring myself by not allowing a few careless individuals to add more pain and disappointment to my life.

Disappointment forms when sadness or displeasure manifests itself, when hopes or expectations are not met. Sometimes the hardest thing to understand or comprehend is when those who we expected to be there during our darkest hour are missing in action when you need them most.

It's really hard to navigate your way through when you're at a weak point and people just pass you by. I don't highlight this so you feel sorry for me, I mention it because I am sure it happens to you too. I am trying to filter between what is down to my poor choices of friendship and what is down to others not stepping up and being dependable when I need them most.

We all fall short and make mistakes, have I always been the perfect friend? No I haven't, but have I always been available and present to those I care about? Yes, I have. The biggest disappointment through my divorce was the amount of people who never showed up, I heard nothing from them and I have mentioned this in a previous chapter, but it hurts and people need to reflect, I am talking about people I had once had an occasional dinner with, whom I thought cared, it's been several years and I still haven't heard from some people. The silence is deafening. Do I miss them? Sometimes, however I do aim to not care because once someone stops caring, I don't suffer fools, so I value the small core of trusted band of brothers and sisters which have helped build me up. Now over time that circle is enlarging but you have to earn my trust and respect.

It's extremely difficult to navigate through this life as a man when there are so many obstacles and situations we find ourselves in and when you think the person who's going to reach out a hand to help you up doesn't even show up, it takes its toll on your soul. So we have to find a way to deal with the disappointment and sometimes that means making difficult choices. Do I think I have hit the sweet spot on how to pick and develop meaningful relationships? Not exactly. But do I reduce the amount of disappointment I face now? Yes, I do. I pick my people wisely. I have some of the dearest friends on the planet, they have good hearts, no judgement just dependable and solid love.

We eventually have to leave the disappointment behind, we have to realise we sometimes elevate people to such a level that they simply can't meet our expectations. I don't believe I ask for much but what I do ask for is rooted in a high standard of friendship. I expect my people to be there when the shit hits the fan. I expect them to have my back, to always back me publicly even if they then disagree with me privately. We have to let go of the past and don't be afraid to lose friendships which are not serving you and honouring you the way you deserve. Friendship is a two-way street. So while I have high expectation, I equally expect me to give to my friends in a very clear and loving way. I will not ask for something from someone that I would not be prepared to give to someone else. My mantra is "If you want a friend, be a friend".

Disappointment really grips our soul when we really needed a person in our hour of need, which doesn't happen that often, only to find they are nowhere to be seen, they are unavailable. Of course, there will be times when a friend simply can't be available to you and that I understand, but being unavailable for a whole season of your life is just unacceptable.

We need to master when to let go of the disappointment, because if we don't we will grow resentful and bitter and neither are pleasant to befriend. I fully embody Jim Rohn's philosophy which speaks of "we are the average of the five people we associate ourselves with." The five closest people to our own lives are the average of our own performance, understanding and ability. One of the most beautiful things to understand is when someone leaves your life, they are actually giving space for someone else, someone new in your life. I think it's a beautiful way to frame a lost relationship, when

119

that person moves out of your life, someone else can take that place. There is always a natural churn when it comes to friendships. Some people will be in your life for a long-extended period and others will be in it just for a season.

It's worth noting that there is a discrepancy between what is down to you and what is down to someone else when it comes to settling on life's differences. We can't change someone's belief but we can adjust our own. Sometimes the problem is not how something is given to me but how I receive it. I know there have been times when I have been offended or upset by what I decided to believe about a situation or what was said which actually did look very different to what that person was meaning to convey. We have to be mindful to make sure we don't injure ourselves by the way we play out or respond to what someone has said because sometimes it's a past wound which triggers our mind to think it's a copy and paste situation and yet that isn't the case. We all need to be mindful of our narrative, I know the way I tell myself how a story is going can cause me harm when the story in reality is being played out to a different tune.

How do you deal with the disappointment of others?

- Be reflective on whether you had an unrealistic expectation of the other person
- Learn to forgive
- Understand it often says a lot about what's going on inside of them
- Be prepared to walk away
- Be willing to talk it through
- Don't put your happiness in the hands of another

Chapter 21 - Self Love

Self-love is a hot topic. It is very prevalent and a key focus point for many especially in the self-development space. With such a surge on peoples mental wellbeing, self-love is seen as essential and has now started to become part of our daily routine. As men, love is something that probably stirs up a number of different thoughts and feelings, during my divorce it was essential to soothe myself while trying to make sense of the various thoughts of self-doubt, shame, frustration and anger of a failed marriage.

Our self-talk often sets the tone to what we do and don't do for ourselves and equally what we do and don't say during the private conversations when we are alone. During times of difficulty especially when you are the part of the problem, the ease in which we minister to ourselves self-love becomes more strained and challenging, but actually during the hardest times of our life that's when we need to demonstrate as much self-love as possible.

Firstly, it's vitally important to define what self-love is and what it looks like to you. One of the ways I show myself self-love is a regular monthly massage, it serves as a dual purpose, to administer care to myself through the power of touch and to relieve stress from my body. Massage is a great way to show self-love to body, mind and spirit.

Self-love is a way to be fully conscious and aware of the acts of love you express to yourself. It could be to cook your favourite meal, play your favourite game, essentially it's really about showing yourself kindness and love especially when you feel you deserve something more negative.

I think it's true for most of us but we are all our worse critic, we tend to be harder on ourselves more than anyone else could be. We need to look at the impact we are having through our negative self-talk and then how we treat ourselves. Self-love is really about accepting yourself as you are and accepting that you deserve love even when you get it wrong or feel unloveable. We have all felt unloveable during the lowest points of our life. Everyone!

My love for my children does not change whether they have been naughty or not, do I get upset and disappointed on occasion when they do wrong, yes I do, but does my love change for them? Nope. It's the same for you and I. Separate between person and actions, you may not agree with the action of someone which does not mean the person is wrong, it just means you don't agree with them. Do I always get it right? No, I don't. Am I still worthy of love? Yes, I am.

Going through a divorce is one of the hardest and most difficult experiences you can face, it's very easy to self-harm yourself emotionally, you berate your every choice and decision, you think about the pain and discomfort you put your children through, it's a hard road and yet I have been able to show myself love, realising I am human, I make mistakes, I get it wrong, but everyone does, forgiving yourself is sometimes harder and takes more time than forgiving someone else.

Self-love can go a little deeper and on occasion maybe confused for being selfish. Self-love means taking care of yourself sometimes before you take care of others. If you frame it correctly, all of us can only give out of what we have. If I make choices for the sake of me, that's going to result in a happier and healthier Mark Sephton. If I am a father to three children they are going to get a better, happier and relaxed daddy if I am able to do some things which show myself love while maintaining my responsibilities and continuing to show love to others.

Self-love basically shows that you respect yourself. It also creates a healthy boundary. When you know your worth then you're less likely to accept shit or contempt from others. I often talk about not prostituting yourself to try and convince someone you're worthy of love or acceptance, if someone doesn't give you love or accepts you for you, I encourage you to walk away from them. You don't need to be a slave to their ways or expectations. When you have a healthy love of yourself, you're able to make better decisions when it comes to relationships. I won't suffer fools or try to convince someone I am worthy of love, you either share love or you don't. Either is fine, just don't be surprised if I walk away from you because you're not what is good for me.

Self-love enables you to soothe yourself, build yourself up, set standards of how you expect to be treated and reduce the amount of negative, self-absorbed people in your life. It's important you don't settle for less. Greg Reid once said "If something feeds you, feed it more, if it eats you, chop it off."

Self-love means creating healthy boundaries for you to decide what is feeding you and building up your energy and what is depleting you by eating away at your energy and resources really needs to be chopped off. Your mental health and soul require this of you. You don't need to feel guilty about protecting your self-love.

Examples of self-love:

- Massage
- Set Boundaries
- Say No without needing to explain yourself
- Forgive yourself
- Mindful whom you associate with
- Live with purpose
- Mindfulness
- Cook your favourite food
- Eat your favourite food

Chapter 22 - Environment

Sometimes we emphasis too much on changing or developing ourselves. I am a huge advocate for self-development and most of my speeches, books, interviews and writings stem from this notion of self-improvement. Of course, this is still very much essential but sometimes we make the fatal error of trying to fit a square peg in a round hole.

You and I will never be great at absolutely everything we do. We all have some things we are great at and other things not so, sometimes we try so hard to be something we are not or continue to work at something which just isn't our cup of tea. It's heart breaking to watch someone desperately try and prove to themselves and others they can do something and when they can't do it to the standard they would like they tend to berate themselves. Instead, I appeal to you to consider is it about your lack of ability or is it simply that the issue is not indeed you it's the environment you live or work in.

Environment my friend is so key especially right now in the world and times we live in. We need to consider if the environment is serving us or not, is it conducive to our production, our happiness and our life fulfilment. Stop trying to wear a jacket which wasn't designed for you. Perhaps your struggle is not with yourself, maybe it's in the environment you find yourself in. It's worth exploring at the very least.

During the first four months that Covid came to this world it became increasingly difficult for me to manage and continue to reach a reasonable level of mental health. The problem was not with me, it was with the environment I found myself in. Having to self-isolate, to be in lockdown where you don't see other people for months on end was torture, it really affected me.

I have a lovely apartment so I am not being critical of where I live, it's more about the fact that I had to stay in my apartment for long periods of time and went days and sometimes weeks without seeing anyone but my children. I needed to get out, I needed to breathe. Over time that became more manageable, it's August now and things are starting to open up.

A few weeks ago I went to Norfolk with my children, that change of environment did my soul good, it invigorated me, it gave me hope, it felt somewhat normal. Other than the addition of wearing a face mask in indoor places the freedom and the open spaces lifted me and for the first time in a long time I felt stronger and invigorated.

Interesting to note but I was the same man in my apartment as I was in Norfolk and yet I felt a million times better, stronger and happier. What had changed? My environment. If you have hit a wall, if you know you're not happy, if something is off, if you have continually looked at yourself as being the problem, please pause and consider your environment. It may be that a small break is all you need or perhaps it will need a significant life change, the place you work, the place you live etc. maybe necessary for you to find yourself again and live out of that abundance.

When I see people trying to fit into other people's expectations and agendas it breaks me. I want you to feel enlightened, I want you to become so mindful and self-aware of the places you find yourself and reflect on whether that environment is the best for you, consider how your work or where you live can impact on your mood, relationships, confidence and fulfilment.

Fulfilment for me is critical, we have one shot at this life, we need to be fulfilled otherwise what have we done with our life? We all know in many scenarios the right environment needs to be right in order for things to grow, it's no different for you and me. The temperature has to be right, the lighting has to be right, there needs to be a food supply. Of course I am talking metaphorically here but you understand what I am getting at.

Albert Einstein himself said "don't expect a fish to climb a tree." Remember who you are and what you were created to be, acknowledge the gifts and talents you have and stay faithful to them, don't become despondent or upset for the limitations you have, we all have them, find your tree and climb it, stop trying to swim when you were born to climb.

Every day is a choice, every day we choose what to put our energy in, we can try until we are blue in the face but some things are about what you're in and not who you are, which is often what is holding you prisoner. Examine what you tolerate in life, I have come to know that whatever I am willing to tolerate in my life is exactly what I get in my life. If I tolerate abuse, I will have abuse in my life, If I tolerate the way someone speaks to me in a bad way, sadly they will keep having permission and the ability to speak badly towards me, the only way that changes is if and when I decide enough is enough, I set my value, I set my boundary, people respect it or I gently move away and so should you.

The importance of assessing your environment:

- Often the issue can be where you are living and working (Environment) which is the problem and not you
- A change of scene can make all the difference
- If you change your environment it can change your perspective
- A different environment creates new opportunities
- You need the right surroundings to blossom and grow

Chapter 23 - Trusted Few

I think when you go through something painful and or private it's important you keep your circle strong and small. I am very much an open book however whenever it comes to the issues of the heart I am very careful whom I confine in and whom I let walk such a journey. One of my favourite proverbs is "don't cast your pearls to swine." Basically this means you don't take something precious (Your heart) and entrust it to pigs (People that don't value who you are or what you have to say).

I have a couple of dear friends whom I share pretty much everything with, through my divorce and other challenges they have listened, strengthened, soothed, supported and created an environment without judgement where I can process, reflect and heal. You need wisdom alongside a willingness to be vulnerable, but I caution you be wise with whom these trusted few are. It has taken me years to know who I am safe and wise to open up to.

The sad reality is, not everyone can be trusted, you can't always trust your family and sometimes you can't always trust your friends. Now I don't mean they are bad people or even that they have any ill intention towards you but sometimes people are what I call "Leaky" they tend to let out personal details to others. When you're going through something painful, you don't need that being spilled out to others even if it is innocent and perhaps even rooted in care.

It is essential you do have a core, perhaps of two to three individuals maximum who you can do life with. People you can walk the most painful of journeys with. We are not islands cut adrift. We are humans and we each need someone to help us navigate the difficulties which life can present on our path.

I believe that as you have a healthier understanding of who you are, you better understand the need to be selective in your friendships and then how close you entrust the secrets of your heart too. I have friends that I love but perhaps they don't have the maturity or ability to help me be what I need when things are particularly sensitive or prickly. I am so thankful that I have not had to process and walk out the pains and challenges of a divorce by myself.

I put a very high standard on friendship. I expect of myself to be all that my friends need me to be, loyal, committed and a willingness at times to be inconvenienced when they have a crisis and need someone at short notice to drop everything and come and help them deal with the problem at hand and process. I guess that's what I expect from my trusted few, the great thing is, they give it happily. They feel honoured to play that part in my life.

Sometimes it appears more difficult for men to build relationships, from the outside I would imagine most men would agree that it seems women connect more easily with other women, but perhaps the depth of connection and friendship from one man to another takes more time. For me I have always been able to connect on a deep level with another man, probably because I know who I am, I am confident in my own skin but know how to express myself without any weirdness.

I do express love to my closest friends which is very natural and real, my ability to do that does play a part in deepening the trust that you have and enables you to journey more closely. One thing I know is that I actually test how much I trust someone in my life by asking myself a simple question. That question is, "Would I entrust this person to look after my children without me being there?" The reason I ask that is because my children are my everything, I love them with all my heart, so If I ask myself that question, can I entrust my children into this person's care and the answer is yes, then I know that they can be trusted with my heart, my pain, my difficulties. I know perhaps this question may not work for you and I will tell you why. There are very few people I would entrust my children to. I am extremely protective, mindful and attentive to their safety and wellbeing.

My two dear friends, my trusted few are such men that I could entrust my children to without reservation. I know they would care, protect and do my kids right. Perhaps it helps they are fathers too but I know how they hold me and what I share with them so preciously they would be able to meet my need of trust when taking care of my children.

If you keep getting hurt in your friendships and relationships, the problem is not in what you share and what you give, it's in who you share and give to which is the problem. We all need someone to confide in, to do life with, to journey with but who that trusted few will be for you needs to be thought out carefully and sometimes takes time, but when you find it, treasure it, prioritise it and never take it for granted. I love my two dear friends like brothers. I would do anything for them as I feel they would also do anything for me.

How to decide who to trust:

- Who's there when you always need them?
- Who tells you what you need to hear over what you want to hear?
- Who demonstrates the same values and ethos as you?
- Who has proved their worth over the years?
- Who genuinely shows you care and concern?
- Who makes an effort with you, checks in on how you are?

Chapter 24 - Take A Break

Whenever we go through something difficult it's essential to honour the space in which we may find ourselves in. There is often a time for everything and really important that when we have been under a high deal of stress or sadness, that we create a small pocket of "coming away and resting awhile." When we have been under siege with emotional trauma, upset and difficulty it does takes its toll on your health and the way you see the world.

In Inside Job I talked about sometimes you have to stop to get ahead. Sometimes to move forward you have to pause. When something consumes you and you meditate on it, after a while it can deplete you of the last bit of sanity or energy you have left. Taking a break from the normal routine, way of living or way of thinking is vital.

Whenever I've been through the rimmer, I have needed to take some time to pause and take a time out. Relationships are the biggest blessing and the biggest curse any of us will experience. When you've been through a breakup or divorce, you just need some time out to reflect, to let your wounds heal, to evaluate and perhaps just prioritise yourself while you gently build yourself up and lick your wounds.

Similar to the importance of having the right environment, taking a break can be a temporary situation rather than a big upheaval of moving home or changing jobs. Taking a break is a small reprieve or short rest bite while you strengthen yourself or wash yourself down. It's a temporary change for a long-term shift. They say that a rest is as good as a change. Not everything has to be radical in order for it to be poignant and significant.

Whenever you go through emotional trauma give yourself the permission to hold that space for grieving and for healing. You need to be able to find an outlet where you can express all that you think and feel without it overwhelming you. If you are reading this and feel it's resonating with you, make a decision, even if it's just for a long weekend, taking some time out to go easy on yourself, the crucial thing here is to make sure you do it.

Whenever we do anything for a long period of time, it will naturally take its toll, the benefit of taking a break and recharging the batteries will help you think clearly and make better choices in the future. It's true to never make a big decision when in a valley. Which basically means don't make a life-altering decision when you're in the middle of a crisis, try and find some safe ground, some foundation in which to build your choices or decision on.

It's worth considering your options when considering some time out from the constant emotional flux you may be feeling when going through something heavy. Sometimes I need that time to myself to be inside my own head and other times I may go spend a few days with my Godfather where I can process and he can ask me questions to help me navigate more efficiently.

Give yourself permission to pause, don't be afraid of stopping or slowing down for a small period of time to gather yourself and your thoughts.

We all have different ways to recharge, there are thousands of ways in which we can do that. For me it's having a massage, its playing a game of football, it's going for a walk, it may look like taking a bath, listening to some music or even playing a video game. I am aware of what I need to breathe and recharge the batteries, sometimes I need quiet and other times I need stimulus. I would encourage you to keep a diary of those things you look to partake in, that afterwards you feel elevated and invigorated. When we know what works for us personally, it's then that you can factor in these meaningful charge points.

Emotional trauma is a very heavy, complex and life changing experience or series of events and we can carry those traumas with us for a long long time, it's at this point where you really need a high degree of self-awareness of what your personal needs are and what your outlet is in order to acknowledge your current need and then meet it. Working with a therapist over the last twelve months has given with an outlet to honour the trauma and then meet it head on in order to continue to process the weight in which it brings us all, thankfully now I have been able to soothe some of my past memories and increase my resilience to those things which continually trouble me.

Importance of taking a break:

- Helps you reset and recharge so you can think clearly and act wisely

- Our mind falls into alpha state when we take time out which helps us be creative
- Protects your body from sickness and stress
- Helps you assess the direction you are going in
- We need to be comfortable when we are not doing anything

Chapter 25 - Lean on God
(Lean on What You Believe in)

I understand when you read the headline of this chapter your response maybe indifferent. Regardless of whether you believe in God or not, or even if you believe in something else, this chapter is still very much worth reading, you can apply elements to your own faith or beliefs, or perhaps just ponder what I share.

My relationship with God is a personal one, I had a personal encounter with God when I was thirteen so that experience is very real to me, in some ways it doesn't matter if you believe in God or not, it won't affect my stance that I do believe because it's a personal experience. We all have our own personal experience of many varying things but to me God has been an anchor and compass when my whole world is at sea.

I must admit trying to settle the conflict inside myself when going through a divorce and the Christian beliefs of divorce being far from encouraged, it's not been easy to reconcile my thoughts and feelings in making the decision to divorce when the Christian faith and knowledge is that God's stance is clear. Thankfully he still loves me but rather than me losing sleep thinking I have done something which God is not pleased with, I think what God is saying when he says "I hate divorce" is really based on how much pain and hurt it causes not only to the people involved but those that are affected by such a decision. It isn't pretty, it is painful, it does have consequences, lives are affected, people's opinions of you do change.

Yet I know that if God's love is perfect, void of error or mistake then regardless of what I do in life, his love is always there for me, while he may not always be happy with my choices or reasons he will love me no matter what. The reason why this has become easier for me to grasp is because I am a father to three incredible children and yet my love for them is not perfect, I do know that even when they do something that upsets me, it does not change the fact that I love them dearly, if I have that stance, viewpoint and heart, how much more will Gods love cover my error, mistakes and choices.

All through my life since I had that personal encounter with God when I was thirteen I have journeyed my deepest fears, concerns and pain and pour myself out in prayer before God, asking him to help, guide and strengthen me. He has been my shelter and listening ear. I have not always felt him close through the many hours, days and weeks of heartache, tears and pain but I have seen his faithfulness and compassion which sometimes is expressed through others and sometimes its expressed through his presence, favour or what could have happened but didn't materialise.

I have always needed at times in my life someone or something which felt bigger than myself. An energy, a person or a belief which was bigger than my human strength or ability, that could ground me, soothe me or comfort me, someone who on occasion looked out for me, had my back, reassured me everything was going to be okay, for me that's the role God plays in my life, someone bigger, wiser and stronger.

My faith has not always been strong, sometimes God seems so distant, so cold that I have wondered at times where God was. I don't have all the answers, all I know is that when I leaned on God I found courage, strength and a resolve to keep moving forward.

I have never had suicidal thoughts but there were times during my divorce where I just wanted the pain in my heart to stop, that if this was all life was to present to me, I would rather not drink from this cup of suffering. I am sure you can relate to the constant pain you feel in your heart if you've ever gone through something so real and raw and you just couldn't seem to find a way out or a way to soothe yourself. I needed something more than what I could find within. I needed something to challenge the loneliness in my heart. While I have had reasonable support and friendships, some paths have to be walked alone. When you go through a divorce such a path exists, that regardless of those around you, it's the one within your very heart which takes the most courage and manifests the post pain, coldness and abandonment. When God is my anchor, he can meet me there like no other and sustain me and help me through.

Those dark days were not pretty, at times I felt I wasn't going to make it, I wasn't going to feel happiness or intimacy again, but I did and I have. God has given me a beautiful woman who has helped put me back together and helped polish some rough edges and deal with some issues within my heart which needed time and attention. We should continue to grow together, no man is an island. God works in many different ways. God is the anchor, just like the earth orbits the sun, we orbit God or what we believe, but God and our belief remain the same but our view changes as we move through life. Let's not lose sight of that as we transition from pain to healing, from confusion to enlightenment.

We all understand our own "Why?" we need to continue to meet ourselves with empathy and understanding for the choices we've made. Whatever is your strength and pillar, lean on it.

Why I lean on God:

- He has always been present in my suffering
- He gives me strength and grace
- He changes my mindset and frames me in a way that releases my anxiety and stress
- It brings me comfort and peace
- He reaches parts of my soul and spirit than no human is able to reach

Chapter 26 - Look Yourself in The Mirror

It's not always comfortable and it's not always easy, to look yourself in the mirror. Sometimes we are happily surprised by what reflects back to us and other times the opposite. Actually, right now just put this book down, and go take a look at yourself in the mirror, take a good look for a few minutes, make observations, look at detail, look at your hair and your face. Just hold yourself in that moment. Okay, now you've done that, reflect on what the general conversation was about, was it critical or encouraging?. Did anything surprise you in a good way? And did anything make you feel uncomfortable or cringe? It's not always easy to look in the mirror but in doing so you can at least have the chance to put something which is off centre, right and something which pleases you can lift your spirits and mood.

Looking in the mirror is actually our friend, it helps us style our hair, brush our teeth, shave our beard, put in contact lenses... you catch my drift. The mirror is your friend even if at times we don't like what we see, it at least gives us an opportunity to correct it before we share ourselves with the outside world. The biggest challenge and yet the most rewarding is the mirror which looks at your heart, your attitude, your character, the way you think and express. This mirror is the one that is often the most painful and yet liberating when you have the courage to really look despite your fear or concern of what it may reveal.

True growth will always be a little painful, it's stretching the limit, it's pushing the boundary, it's taking on new form, it's enlarging your capacity, there is a stretching which happens when we grow. Sadly, if you want to grow, you're going to have to look yourself in the mirror and accept and acknowledge some of what is looking back at you isn't pleasant, attractive or desirable. Be encouraged though, once you know the problem and the challenge you can go get some help or insight of how to change the picture.

My mirror this year has been in the shape of a psychologist. This was my choice, something I had considered for the past year and when Covid hit, it kind of created an opportunity and heightened my need to get some help, to add some new tools to my already comprehensive tool kit. Being isolated and staying home forced my hand to get help, to look at some of my triggers and flaws and see if I could oust them from my mind and soothe the painful reaction I would find myself in.

I know many men who will not entertain opening up their hearts, their past and their pain to anyone. So we all have a choice. I know for me I would rather face the pain so I can move beyond it than feel it hiding in some dark corner but never ridding myself of it. Regardless of shame, disappointment, anger, sadness or whatever negative emotion it is, I want it out of me if it's not serving me, if it's not helping me be a better man, better father, better partner, better son, better brother, better uncle and a better friend.

The issues on this occasion was not about what the problems or challenges I faced but really how to overcome them, how to pause without reacting, how to soothe myself, how to keep a level of control without self-imploding or self-harming emotionally. I do believe that more and more of us self-harm emotionally even more so than physically. I know when my relationships have been off with people it has caused me to be so self-critical, that I take full responsibility for why there is an issue and then I convince myself that I am the bad one, that it must be something I have done or said. The reality is, it's not always been about me, if at all. It's been about them and yet I have in the past internalised that the reason why such and such is distant with me is because of something in me, newsflash – it's actually about what's going on inside them. Once I changed my narrative and the story I kept telling myself, the negative emotions no longer attached themselves to blame and I found I had more understanding, compassion and hope for the other person.

It's clear to me that over the years I have had abandonment issues, fears of rejection and being cut off from those I love. It has sometimes caused me to react in a not so charming way where my behaviour may be deemed as controlling, not something I am proud to admit, but controlling for the sake of me preventing myself from the fear of rejection and abandonment I have so dreaded stimulating from my parents breakup when I was a child.

We all know that any controlling behaviour in a relationship is going to cause problems and often the thing you fear becomes reality but not for the reason you thought, it's almost like you create self-sabotage, when you control a partner they can become stifled and feel like they can't

143

breathe, it takes a very understanding and compassionate partner to work with you on such issues. Thankfully I have such a partner and together we've been able to soothe and remove large parts of that behaviour and demonstrated trust and honesty, while also providing assurances and clarity. This has helped alongside the power of changing my narrative. What I mean by that is the story you tell yourself. For example, rather than telling yourself that your partner may cheat on you, the narrative changes to my partner loves me and she has chosen to be with me for a reason, relax in that, who you are to her is very different to who a friend of hers can be to her. We each have our own space when it comes to relationships.

Do you like what you see? Don't you like what you see? And why? Pick up a pen and answer that. Make a real conscious point of this question. Pause and be honest about yourself. The point of looking in the mirror is both for your emotional and physical wellbeing and sake. We need to be mindful if we find ourselves being heavily critical and emotionally berating ourselves for choices we've made, we run the risk of self-punishment and we need to be more gentle for the times we may have got things wrong, we often never mean to cause the pain and sorrow that sometimes is inflicted on others.

I realised after some time of retrospection that divorce itself is not the biggest harm to our children, it is actually the conflicts that parents have which cause children the most harm, it's about the environment. You can pat yourself on the back if you never divorced but instead your children experienced something more harmful than if you had actually separated. When our behaviour as parents becomes unpredictable I would argue that this is what causes children the most pain and the main issues compared to two people deciding this isn't working and jointly make the transition and create two positive separate environments for children to live, play and grow.

I want to mention the importance of boundaries while focusing on looking in the mirror, once we take a good look at ourselves one of the things to consider is whether we have healthy and strong boundaries in our relationships, boundaries are as equal to keep things in as much as they are to keep things out. The majority of us will have a fence of some sort, we have a fence around our property which highlights our territory, it helps neighbours know what is theirs and what is yours. Having healthy boundaries ensures that you are protecting your own energy, value and time. When we look in the mirror we become more conscious of our needs, we start to understand our own limitations and boundaries, these are to help you not only manage but also to excel and ensure that those people that you love most and those things that are most valuable to you are met with the highest sense of self, rather than spread thin. It's here that I encourage you to be selfish, that if you have had enough sleep you're actually going to be a better parent or partner, rather than thinking I can't say no to this and that, by saying no, you actually preserve yourself.

Why you should look yourself in the mirror:

- It helps you reflect and evaluate your current behaviour, vision and actions
- Because the only person who we really fail in this life is ourselves, we need to take a look in the mirror so

145

we can make the important adjustments to improve our performance

- It's vitally important to know who you are and who you are not, and make decisions based on that revelation
- You can't see the growth or the development if you have nothing to measure it by, when we look ourselves in the mirror we can see the improvements as well as the areas which may need attention

Chapter 27 - Grieve

Often when we go through grief or turmoil we don't always give it the space it needs to express itself, to find an opportunity to let out or express the pain but it's so so important that we do grieve for those things that have been lost, misplaced, absent or missing. Sometimes grief can be temporary and a change of circumstance can present a quick and swift end to grief. The grief I am talking about is the one which is much more final. The death of a loved one is pretty final at least for the rest of this life on earth. When we lose someone we love there needs to be time to grieve, heal and just be sad. It doesn't weaken the memories by grieving. It's very much a necessity to grieve when you experience loss. I would say as a whole, men are not as good at grieving as women, but I want to caution men, if you don't express and get a release from your grief or indeed any negative emotion it will make you sick, either mentally or physically, emotions need to find expression.

We have to honour and frame grief in the correct way, as we do with all emotions. They are not always pleasant to experience or indeed feel, but they are still a feeling and an emotion which are not alien to man. As I have said already, there is a difference between wallowing and then sitting in something, the key is to let it have its time and then move on as best you can. Grief is a strong intense emotion, it isn't pleasant but it's not bad. What is bad is not letting it have its space and time. Once you've let out the emotion, the pain and the sadness, then it's time to frame it in a positive way which gives you joy and strength rather than fear and sadness, of course that takes time, but when you let it be, that process moves a lot quickly.

Last year I lost my grandma, she was ninety-six when she passed away, she lived a long and full life. I admire her for many reasons, my gran was one of a kind and I cherish many memories which actually came in the last two years of her life. I guess when you consider old people in your life and when you consider grandparents that enter the latter stages of life, you become fully aware that their time on earth is shortening by the day. So even at times when I started to see my gran deteriorate and even though there is an expectation that she will soon leave the earth, nothing really prepares you for the loss and grief you experience when the person you saw faithfully every Thursday for the past two years is suddenly not here. I had to honour the grief I felt, not being able to see her when I wanted, not to listen to her stories or listen to Frank Sinatra together in the conservatory, all those sorts of things are no longer an option. I had to grieve for her absence. For the pure fact she isn't here on earth now, I have one last grandparent in my family. I gave myself time to grieve, I honoured that grief by writing a memoir at her funeral and sharing it before my family. Little small expressions like that help you grieve. Acknowledging the pain helps, talking it through and having a personal space to honour someone's life is so so important. It could be that you've lost someone that you love, it happens to us all. It's just significant and beneficial that you let that out.

The other grief we can experience is that of a divorce, the marriage, happiness and love you once had can now be long gone, it can sting. Even if you've reconciled it's the right path to take, what you once had is no longer there. The hardest two things when I went through my divorce was no longer living in my family home and not waking up to my kids every single day. I grieved those two facts every day for about twelve months and eventually I became reconciled with the reality of my situation but I grieved the absence of two things I held dearly and now I needed to take the grief and create a new normal and find happiness in a new way, and as I write this and reflect on how I feel and how things are now, I have managed to reach a place within my heart where I am ok with it. I have found a way through, it wasn't easy, it took longer than I would have liked but the grief was essential in order for me to find the healing I have now. The deeper the wound, the more necessary it will be for you to grieve and to let that out of your system before you can even entertain finding a place within your heart that feels slightly normal.

My life has been full of loss as I am sure yours has too. I am not bitter, I am not in a victim mindset, do I complain and hurt sometimes? Yes, I do. Am I mindful that some of my suffering and grief can be self-induced, yes, I am mindful of that. Some things in life you will get back, you will recover and find a new way of happiness. Sadly, none of us can bring back a loved one from the dead and while you can't get back everything, you can find energy and hope and satisfaction in the future. I dream I will create a new family home where I am with all those I love and an environment which makes me feel like an accomplished happy and family-orientated man that I know I am. We can't reach that point until we grieve over the very things we used to have, until then I will run the risk of growing bitter and sadly sick. If you've had a lot of sickness in the last twelve months be mindful and reflect on what the condition of your relationships are and if you need to express emotions in order to bring your body back into full health.

Sometimes it's important to stay in the emotion and limit it, the reason we limit it, is so we can recharge, it gives us a chance to increase our self-care and hold a place for ourselves to process. Grief shows you that you had love for that person or situation, we should all be grateful for the process of grief because after all, life is a process of love and you can't have one without the other. Life is dynamic, it is constantly moving ahead, and so we must. We must acknowledge the transitions of life and do our best to not be left behind. It takes bravery to stay in the pain, it's okay to feel whatever you do, grief is complex. Find beauty in the imperfection. Either you express the emotion, or grief will express itself inside you, you get to choose. Choose wisely. It's so important to keep looking ahead.

We are all guilty of it and yet I believe its permissible for one reason and one reason only, otherwise I encourage you to stop looking backwards to what you once had, how life used to be. The only time we should look back on how our life used to be in comparison to how it is now, is purely to see the growth you can see by measuring where you were, to where you are now, otherwise don't do it. If you feel life was better and you were better in the past compared to your present it won't actually help you or aid you, if anything it will depress you and short circuit that which is ahead of you.

The reality is often our situation and circumstances change over the course of time and so therefore it's not fair to yourself to compare how you and life was when you were eighteen-years-old, compared to when you are thirty-nine. When I was eighteen I had very little responsibility, I had a job but I lived with my dad and sister, I didn't have anyone to worry about but myself, I was on my own schedule, I had my own money and other than car expenses I didn't have the financial or relationship responsibilities that I do now. When all I had to think about was me, it's easy to fall into the trap that life was easier and I was happier than I am now purely because my situation was different. It's not useful or helpful for you or I to compare how we were and how our life was back then, when so much of our life is different now.

I find we all at some point try to go back to how things were, but the magic is in what's ahead, not what is behind. I need you to grasp this very concept because it's what will set you free. You keep trying to go back to the person you were, the way you used to look, the way you used to feel, the way life was easier, happier, more simpler. You're trying to retrace your steps in the hope you can tap back into that one moment in time, where life made sense and you felt great. I remember when I was eighteen and I had all the time in the world, I could pray for hours, I could play computer games for hours, I could sleep when I wanted, I could eat when I wanted, I could do what I wanted. Now I have three amazing children, I have clients, I have responsibilities, while I do have a lot of time, freedom due to me being my own boss, I can't keep comparing the two very different stages of my life and neither can you.

Don't lose hope for what you want, I want you to be happy, fulfilled, motivated and feeling like you are living out of your sole purpose, but the way to get there is not going backwards, its moving forward. It's focusing on what is ahead. Don't keep working to go back to where you were, go forward with what's ahead, don't go back, understand the process of change. Your happiness is not to be found in yesterday, it's to be found in the here and now, today.

As time goes by, we all become a little older, which equates to our bodies potentially not looking as good as they used to, even our minds cannot fire as responsively as they could in our twenties. Whatever the reason for why you compare and look back on your past it's often not the key to help shift you out of your current doldrum. The key here is to schedule some soul time for yourself, take an hour, schedule a meeting with yourself and head to a quiet place in your home, turn off all distractions and sit with yourself with a pen and paper, write down how you are feeling, name those feelings and emotions and try to make more sense of why you feel them, then focus on the feelings and emotions you want to feel and give some thought as to how some of these emotions and feelings maybe stirred up in a positive way, but make sure you do this exercise where you are looking forward, looking to the horizon and not the shadows of the past.

If we continue to look behind, we will not grab hold of what we want, we will only find more heartache and frustration. If we look for what's ahead, we will find what we are looking for. We are all trying to solve a puzzle, but we must not forget that you are a piece of that puzzle and the way to change your current situation and mindset is to look ahead, not behind, go after what is in front of you. It's time to move on.

Why it's important to grieve:

- We all need to release emotion otherwise it has the power and ability to make you sick
- When we grieve see it as a way of honouring the person or circumstance that has been lost
- It helps you move forward and deal with challenges in the future
- Losing something hurts, it's normal to grieve

Chapter 28 - Accept What You Can't Change

It's funny, whenever I read "Accept what you can't change" I feel both liberated and frustrated at the same time. Let me explain, I am frustrated because I like to be able to change everything, I love choice and I love the ability to decide for myself, I don't like being told what to do and I don't like not having choices. I like options and I even like to create my own options. If I don't want to do something I won't do it, guilt will not drive me, I don't have a problem saying no. If I really don't want to do it then I won't. Very simple. That's why "Accept what you can't change" is something that I find difficult and yet sometimes the only way I have found peace or a way out is to accept things the way they are even though I don't choose them or even want them.

I hated the lockdown for that very reason. Not because I don't want to be responsible, I have always been responsible and smart and I would never intentionally do something which would put another human in danger, but I just don't like freedom being taken away, if you are educated and have common decency you should be able to decide what is best for you and for those around you, granted not everyone is as sensible as you and I.

The first four months of lockdown due to Covid was brutal for the very reason I mention, very few choices were available to me, I couldn't play football, I couldn't see friends, I couldn't watch a game of football, I couldn't hug my family, I couldn't go to the gym etc. You get the drift, it affected you the same way too. I battled with it so hard, the last thing I wanted to hear is another person say, "we are all in the same boat." Nope we are not in the same boat, we are in the same storm. My boat, my needs and my choices are a lot different to yours. It's irrelevant really because when you go through something like that, you're the one who has to make sense of it and navigate your way through. Lockdown was a blessing for some and a curse for others.

I don't like to admit or accept I can't change something. My very last resort if I have a choice is to accept I can't do anything about it. I am a man who doesn't always take no as no apart from when its relational and then I accept someone's boundary. I don't always accept no when for example I am annoyed about some poor customer experience and they say they can't do anything about it and then as soon as I escalate it something gets done about it.

I am not a man who accepts things if I don't think justice or fairness is being served, so you can see how frustrating accepting a lockdown was, not because it didn't make sense, not because I didn't understand the importance to my own health and safety and the safety of those around me, not even because I believe I am invincible because I don't, but because I could have navigated my way through a better way than what the UK government blanketed the whole country to do. For a person's mental health the road they took was costly to many.

It's one thing for me to have to accept choices for myself and sometimes accept those things I can't change, it's no truer when it comes to relationships. Some people are so bad at relationships that sadly you can get caught up in the middle of them, because the reality is you can't change someone else and you certainly can't control what they think, say and do. That's difficult. I want the best for my life and in order to have the best for my life I want my relationships to be strong, healthy and real and when they are not, it hurts.

Relationally too often I have taken responsibility for issues which are actually not about me but about what's going on in the other person. I have caused myself hurt and pain by internalising another's behaviour and choice and held myself responsible. It's not right to do that, the issue is with them, I have to accept I can't change what and who they are even if I wish it were different so I could have the relationship I would like with them.

Accepting what I can't change here is what I find liberating and not so much frustrating. I am responsible for me and you are responsible for you. I have to accept the way our relationship is or I have the choice to discard it, it's not always easy but that the truth of the matter, you do get the matter of choice, you just have to choose wisely.

They say that acceptance is sometimes what you have to do in order to deal with something or find healing in something. It may be accepting something you don't really want or you desperately wish were a different way, when you accept, the war within you resides and you can at least start to find some closure and some rest to just to surrender to what is. It isn't easy. It's hard to accept things that are not quite the way you want them to be but once you do, you can start to reframe and look for the positives and opportunities to work with what you have.

Lockdown stopped me doing many things, but I had to find new things to do. Things that would stimulate me and give me a sense of purpose, purpose is key when the choices are few and far between. So I decided one day during lockdown to walk 50,000 steps in a day and I did it, in fact I did 57,000 steps which equated to some 25 miles. It felt liberating to achieve something. If I can find substitutes to choices and options I certainly will. I started learning a new language, I started walking a minimum of 20,000 steps a day. I was doing all I could to shift my mood, stabilise my mental health, it just really became tricky when there were certain things you could no longer do, like hug your family and friends which made it much more difficult to deal and cope with. My mental health took a battering as it did for many.

Acceptance isn't always easy and it doesn't always fit hand-in-glove, on the contrary but when nothing you do or say, wish or hope for changes or shifts the outcome then you will sit in frustration and barrenness a long long time, however if you accept the not-so-favourable options and choices because to be fair you can't do anything about your situation, relationship or circumstances right now, then accepting brings you the power back, you now are taking responsibility again for yourself, where you focus your time and energy and the way you look at things.

Accepting allows you to work with what you have, affect what you can, put your sole focus into those things that can be changed, can be altered and can be improved. Sometimes a part of life is accepting that which we don't really want and see if we can change our narrative towards it or if needs be reject it and walk away, but even walking away doesn't give you what you really want and perhaps with time, things will shift and start moving around to the way you want them, but don't hold your breath.

Why it's important to accept what you can't change:

- You become frustrated, angry and bitter in trying to change something you have no power to be able to
- Acceptance helps you deal and shows you the road to take
- Because there are plenty of things you can change which need your time and energy which they can't have if you are so focused on the things you can't change
- It's helpful to know not everything is our choosing or wish and that's okay, we just need to work with what we have
- Francis of Assisi prayed "Lord grant me the serenity to accept the things I can't change, the courage to change the things I can and the wisdom to know the difference".

Chapter 29 - Foundations Rocked

It's very hard when the very core of your foundations are rocked by the occasional turbulence we all experience at some time in our lives, it's hard to steady the ship when time and time again, wave after wave, we experience continual problems that seem to batter down upon us when we are at our most vulnerable.

The majority of our foundations lay within the basics, our health, our relationships, our finances and our purpose, these are our basic foundation I would say, whenever these come under siege it's hard to stabilise and refocus ourselves but it's vitally important that we have the ability and necessity to calm the waters when all hell breaks loose.

Our ability to stay grounded and centred when at our core we are experiencing enemy invasion which may look like a relationship breakup, an unplanned financial cost or a trip to the doctor which reveals bad news. Whatever it is, we must find a way to find fresh perspective and face the problem head on, burying your head in the sand is not an option, it doesn't deal with the problem and eventually it will overwhelm you and wipe you out.

I am very mindful to accept and adopt the stories that others believe especially if they have a negative viewpoint, however one thing which always seems to be true based on experience is often bad things come in threes. I don't know why, I certainly don't welcome one bad thing let alone three but it does seem to happen. When life gets like that it's very hard to remain calm let alone positive.

When your world is turned upside down what do you do? What is your point of reference of dealing with difficulties, if you don't know? It would be worth pausing here and taking some time to think about what you do or don't do when your foundations are under siege.

I certainly know from my time of going through the divorce process much of your foundation is rocked, lots of familiarity almost overnight becomes alien to you, the place you once lived you know longer do, the person you once slept beside you know longer do, the family gatherings as you've known them stop, waking up to your children every morning stops, the way people treat you and interact with you, relationally my world was rocked. I was also mindful of the reality that it wasn't just my foundations under siege but it was my children too. That's where most of mine and my ex-wife's efforts went, to protect the children, to validate them and to reassure them, I would say overall we've done a pretty good job of that.

Life is a serious business, seldom do we hear the real stories which go on in people's lives, very rarely do we get to see or hear what happens in the four walls which we call home and in some cases that's probably for the best, but in order for us to really impact and strengthen each other and for this book to even change one man's life there has to be some honesty and some real talk which takes place over the course of these pages.

Life is tough, as a man I believe it's as tough as it can be, some of that is our own doing. Men don't always choose well or speak well or act well and that's why we end up with some of the difficulties we face, we are our own worst enemy, other times it's a question of how we deal with the unjust and unfair realities which land on our lap because we live in an unperfected world full of ego driven, selfish and power-hungry individuals.

When our foundations are rocked we must not turn to things which do not solve the problem, if it helps solve the problem then give it your attention, if it doesn't solve the problem the reality of it is it probably isn't what's best for you and in some cases can make things worse.

We know all too well that people fall into addictions when dealing with life problems, the problem is it doesn't take them away or fix them, it just gives a temporary distraction until that feeling or situation rears its ugly head again. Let's be mindful of where we go or what we do when we are under siege, when the pressure is on, when there is pain in our heart, where do we go? And what do we do?

I do love the game of poker, I love the strategy and I love the risk, I also know it's a form of gambling when you play for money, I don't really drink and I don't have any other vices, I have never been interested with any other form of betting, it's that particular game I like and enjoy the social aspect of playing with friends. I am mindful of the risk and my reaction when I don't win. If I am brutally honest when I lose I don't always like the way I feel or even how I act and behave. So I am extremely mindful that this can happen and so I have to assess why that is. From self-reflection I know I have a high degree of justice, I do understand that playing cards is a win or lose outcome, so I am not deluded however I do get upset if I play nine hands and lose all nine hands, then I get vexed. I am sure I am not the only one at some point in playing a game there seems to be a conspiracy against you winning!

I am mindful that when I have gone to play poker as a means to cheer myself up, rarely does that work and in more cases than not it actually tends to make you feel worse. So now when I am not in a good place emotionally I actually stay away from playing. I have determined it's only right I play when I am in a good place emotionally and then I find I enjoy it a whole lot more. The funny thing is, when you need it less you tend to win more.

People have a split opinion on any form of gambling, in some ways I have a hard time when people say "Mark likes to gamble." I just like the game. I am mindful as to my reasons why I play and I have reconciled that I play for the right reasons which are because I enjoy it, I enjoy the strategy and the risk and I love the social side, do I understand the risks in playing? Yes I do, but just like the difference between having a glass of wine or drinking the whole bottle a lot of it comes down to why and how much.

I share this so vulnerably because we all have something we go to which may or may not help serve us and when our foundations are rocked we look for some comfort, some escape or some pleasure. Some ways out are less harmful than others or have less consequences when we partner with them, however it's much healthier to understand and reflect on the mechanisms or enjoyments we have and see if they really help serve or just hinder our current challenges.

As a rule of thumb I tend to set out and do the hard thing first, I tend to prioritise my day and my challenges by asking myself the question "If I only achieved one thing today what would it be?" That tends to be my focus. If I have a problem or challenge I tend to use the same principle, what one thing could I do today which will make the biggest difference to this challenge or current problem. I have shared before that I always sleep on a problem, I encourage you all to follow your gut and don't deviate from your true values, that way even if you make a wrong choice it won't break you, you will just need to reset.

When it comes to difficulties in your life one of the hardest things to master and yet if you master it, it shall be your greatest asset is the ability to know the difference between distraction and direction. At times we can do something which either distracts us from the problem which may or may not be best depending on the situation or we have a clear direction of what we need to do to rectify a problem. At times it's good to completely shift the energy away from the problem and often a period of pause or focusing our attention on something else can actually help, for when we return to the problem we have renewed energy from engaging in something different or we have a new perspective as we all tend to look at things differently when we come from a place of strength rather than from a place of frustration and tiredness.

I have seen those closest to me who have several problems, these are real problems but they think by distracting themselves these problems will magically disappear, rarely does this happen, if anything the problem gets worse. I don't tend to let things become worse for me, so it's painful and difficult to see when those around me don't realise the increased harm they are causing themselves by burying their head in the sand in the hope the problem goes away. None of us can conquer what we won't confront. So stop hiding from the truth. Yes, sometimes the truth is painful, uncomfortable and even heartbreaking but we must take direction and not use distraction to overcome the majority of our problems. We must break the problem down and do one small action each day to overcome and eradicate the issue from our life.

What to do when your foundations are rocked:

- Never make a major decision in a valley
- Stay grounded and don't do anything crazy that you may later regret
- Centre yourself and have a few trusted friends rally around you
- Remember the situation is temporary and not permanent
- Re-evaluate and take stock of the situation, then make practical baby steps to address the issue at hand

Chapter 30 - Finding Beauty
in The Imperfect

I was recently speaking to a dear friend of mine. We often meet up to discuss matters of the heart and do life together. It's so important we have the ability and opportunity to create our own community where we can share those things which mean something to us and also those things which weigh heavy on our heart.

During one of these recent and familiar heart-to- hearts with my friend the coin of phrase "Finding beauty in the imperfection" was very apt and resonated with me.

Life for all of us is a mosaic of the brutal and beautiful. We often find ourselves right in the middle of these polar expressions.

I don't know about you but it seems life has become more and more challenging. We are more stressed and anxious than ever before. While I live in reality and the here and now, I have always looked to the horizon for the next best thing to enter my life and when it's hard to see the more positive things on the horizon it can leave you feeling flat. I like my business, relationships and life to have some kind of order, some kind of attraction and development and the gulf between where I am and where I want to be is where the unrest of my heart can dwell.

The idea of finding beauty in the imperfect seemed a little profound to me and so I decided to chew on it, reflect and meditate on this notion that there is beauty in our mess, in our pain, in our suffering and in our transition from where we are to where we want to be and even more importantly who we are and who we want to be.

I have always wanted more, not of objects or material things but I have always wanted more from life and more notably from myself. I want to keep growing and evolving and I can sometimes become frustrated with myself and my situation as I find the best way to express the true likeness of who I really am.

So how do we find beauty in the imperfection? How do I practically and mentally do that? I have always been one to try and overcome a challenge, I have a fair degree of stubbornness which runs through my veins and I want everything yesterday. I am pretty sure that could ring true for you too.

–   Acceptance. Accepting where you are in life and realising you have what you have based on the choices you make (Some exceptions of course) but if we really look at our life, our situation is often based on the small everyday choices to the more life changing ones that we are responsible for, where we live, what job we do etc. Acceptance often brings us empowerment. We become at peace with ourselves when we just accept where we are in life and look to make small steps to improve and evolve in our quest for more fulfilment.

- Process. T.D. Jakes said, "You can't have progress without process." Meaning some lessons in life we can't bypass. There is wisdom, growth and knowledge in the process. People dislike "Mondays" so much and yet the only way to the "weekend" which people love, is to go through Monday to get to it. Sometimes we have to go through the ugly and the painful e.g. childbirth to have a positive result (a baby).

- Gracious with yourself. For me this is probably the most important and the one I struggle with the most. I always expect more and better from myself, I always want to outperform myself, I want to live the best I know how. I want to do everything with heart or not at all. The need for us to realise that what we may be going through in life is stressful, difficult and problematic without feeling the need to embrace shame and guilt when perhaps we haven't dealt with a situation with excellence and so become highly critical of our own behaviour or performance. We must accept when we are doing our best and accepting at times sometimes our best is not enough and that's okay.

- Mindset shift. Everything is won and lost within our minds. Our ability to rule our mind is the most critical component to the way we see the world and ourselves. Our mind is what will lead us to our greatest achievements and our worst nightmares. We are all on a journey of self-discovery. Finding beauty in the imperfection comes from us shifting our minds to one of criticism to self-care and extending grace to our imperfections and moving from the not quite there yet to the realm of I have nailed it.

We need to know that where we are right now is not where we are going to be tomorrow, next week or next year. Depending on how well life is going that could be me throwing you a bone or giving you a reality check that life fluctuates between the beautiful and the brutal but when it is of the more brutal variety that's when we all need to find the beauty in the imperfection, in the pain and in the struggle. Be encouraged, take two minutes to consider where you are in life and how you feel and while your family, business and life maybe missing key components you can still find little pockets of beauty.

Life keeps moving forward, so the small choices we make every day do matter and they do count. Rome wasn't built in a day, focus on the bricks and not the fortress. Focus on the beauty in the imperfect. Establish a routine and stick to it, create spontaneity within your routine and take back control. Appreciate there is always a gulf between where you are and where you want to be.

Chapter 31 - Begin Again

It's actually the title of a movie which I really love featuring Kiera Knightly and Mark Ruffalo. They both are trying to start life over after a very difficult and problematic beginning which includes relationships, finances, work, family and drink problems, on this occasion it's music that saves them, heals their hearts and makes them create something beautiful. I think that's why I love the movie because it's believable and you see elements of it played out in everyday life. The beauty of it is despite the pain and the challenge of it, it does eventually shift from negative energy to positive energy and things work out through a mosaic of the brutal and the beautiful.

Life is messy, it's not always pretty, it's not always rainbows and sunshine. It's often the very opposite of what we really want it to be. The point I really want to drive home with this book is it's not where you start, it's not even the middle, it's really how you finish. We have all been gifted this one life and we must decide how we want to live it and what is the most important when it comes to life choices. They say we are born twice, once when we are physically born and twice when we realise what we were put on earth to do.

It takes courage to start over, to pick yourself up, to dust yourself down, to soothe your own soul and allow God to play his part too. It takes time and it's vitally important that we go easy on ourselves as we transition and pigeon step through the mess we sometimes find ourselves in. Life can be hard and life can be simple. It has its highs and it has its lows and the key really is despite either side of the spectrum we do our level best to stay grounded, calm and brave at all points.

We must sometimes sit with our pain, not to wallow in it, not to let our situation consume us but sometimes to help figure things out, to help find perspective, to even give us strength, sometimes we just have to pause and stop the thrashing around and take some deep breaths. While starting over and beginning again isn't easy, you can also look upon it as a new beginning, a fresh new canvas, an opportunity to put into place the life you always wanted.

You are never going to win everyone over especially when you've been through something like a divorce but the main thing is for you to be at peace with yourself, it's out of that place where people will start to reconnect with you as you find your way forward. Whatever state you find yourself in, however you're feeling and or whatever you are thinking, you can begin again and you must begin again if you've reached a point of defeat and sadness and you can't seem to make sense of life. Honour the pain and the heartache for what it is, it shows you cared but then after a season of time, it's time to go again and create a new normal.

As I sit here today am I where I want to be, am I the man I want to be? In all honesty I am not in the fullness of the man I want to be or even feel the fullness of where I am at this stage of my life, but am I on the right track and have I begun again? Yes, I most certainly have. I am thankful for it, it's only helpful looking behind to give you courage that everything works out and to remind you of what you don't want to happen again, otherwise it's time to create a new future, get clear on what is most important to you, my darling babies and my darling girl are what really matters to me, beyond that it's my dear friends and rest of my family and trying to be as faithful to the gifts that God has given me in the hope they may see a glimpse of who God is through the way I live my life.

While I acknowledge there is a gap between the man I am now and the man I want to become, I also have to weigh and be balanced to the fact that I have established key values at my core which are good and strong and coherent with the man in which I want to be, I want to be in the fullness of the man I know I am capable of being. I am encouraged and must honour the man I am right now, as you must too. I have established true and important principles especially for my children, my partner and those that I love that at the very core of me I am setting myself up to be the best version of myself.

My life is far from perfect, like I said, life is messy but it's held together and protected by God's grace, as we walk this earth we gradually become more enlightened by who he is and the way he relates to us and often we think God is punishing us for past wrongs, he isn't. God is not mean, he's a God of love and he's helped me through many difficult situations. Thankfully none of us really get what perhaps we deserve. Having faith in something bigger than ourselves absolutely helps in beginning again. Whether you believe in God or not, you must find a support network and a community which helps protect you and strengthen you, sometimes we are our own worst nightmare, sometimes we need someone to actually step in and protect us from ourselves.

How to begin again:

- Just take small baby steps, done is better than perfect
- Make some solid choices and stick to them
- Focus on one basic fundamental at a time
- Continue to do what you love and what excites you

Chapter 32 - Patience

After I had decided to discuss the contents of this book with my girlfriend it was apparent that "Patience" was a chapter which was missing, she believed it was very important to highlight and mention. On reflection I think she is right but I also admit I had a good chuckle. The truth is gentlemen, women 100% without fail test your patience, and before all you women start attacking me, I am sure you could argue a good case that we have the same effect on you but in very different ways.

I joke periodically that I am perfectly impatient, I often think it's how we frame things, I argue the point that I am not impatient, I am just hungry, driven and enthusiastic. Perhaps I am just saying that to make myself feel better. I honestly admit I want things yesterday. If I want something in my life, I tend to want to have it now, otherwise, why would I want it? I know from experience often things are worth waiting for but it's not easy to sit back when you're such a go-getter.

I honestly believe the hardest things to be patient for are typically the things which are totally out of your control, getting another human being, in particular your partner, isn't always easy. What may take me a minute, may take my partner an hour. It really depends on what it is as to whether it's worth a fight or a complaint over. Often it isn't. You actually save yourself a lot of stress in just letting things be, but for a man who always loves to effect change, speed things up and be efficient that's not always easy.

I do know that if I had received certain things in life too soon, I actually wouldn't have managed them well, they may have actually caused me harm or perhaps even loss. Often when people win the lottery they end up bankrupt because they don't know how money works, they don't know how to budget, they don't know how to double it, invest it and or protect it, so they squander it. The right gift and opportunity at the wrong time can turn out to be a hinderance and a failure rather than a blessing and a success.

We each have to value the process of time, it takes real skill and wisdom as to when to accept things and keep your peace and when to put a bit of pressure on a person or process to speed things up. When taking your lady on a date it's often in your best interests to let her have all the time in the world, I know I have never regretted it because even though she is naturally beautiful, when I have given her the time to enhance and radiate her already beautiful appearance she feels so much more confident and happy and she makes me look even better than what I did before. So I have learned to give the woman some space, the only tricky part is if you have a reservation and I absolutely hate being late, so I have to manage that by often telling her a slighter early time to what is reality or I encourage her to start getting ready way before I could even imagine it would take.

I mean this is really a silly example but it is something that can cause stress and tension trying to get your partner out of the door. It's worth noting I am a big fan of home dinner dates and then that way you don't run into the same problems!

Patience is defined as having the capacity to accept or tolerate delay, problems, or suffering without becoming annoyed or anxious. That definition is very clear and defined, when holding it up against your own life or what you thought patience meant it's apparent why I as a man struggle with it. I would say it manifests more annoyance in me over anxiety, though I can still identify feeling anxiety when I expected something to be sooner than when it is, perhaps that maybe something like a phone call from a loved one, when you expected them to call that evening and it ends up being days sometimes that can cause me anxiety wondering what the delay or problem is. I admit I have a harder time when things are unknown even over things that are unpleasant to hear.

If the perimeter of patience is having the capacity or ability to tolerate delay or problems it's no wonder as men we struggle with it. It's also part of the reason why the world in which we live in now is to actually prevent delay but the fallout of that is perhaps we've lost the heart of being patient, when we see and experience how easy and functional much of our world is through technology perhaps that's why now more than ever we find such an unrest to wait for anything, indeed this could be another factor why relationships break up at the first sign of a problem, we've lost the ability to accept and tolerate when things don't go to plan, but it could also indicate an issue with selfishness and even ego if we are not able to be reasonable, gracious and accommodating of events or problems which at times, let's be honest, we all face.

I feel the ability to master patience isn't an overnight lesson, I don't even think it's a lifetime lesson, perhaps none of us can be patient all the time and I would even argue there is a time to not be patient, sometimes we suffer for too long, putting up with far too much messing about that being patient can cost us too, but for the majority the need to have patience will serve you and me better.

I believe it's hard for me to be patient in the areas which I find easy, or that I have the answer to or in fact I never have had that particular problem with. I find it frustrating when I know how the process works but you are part of a system which doesn't even know as much as you. What I mean is when your knowledge is greater than a person you're working with, living with or dealing with and yet they want to tell you how to do it and you're just like, "get out of my face you clown."

Whenever patience is needed, it is often about the contrasting needs you each may have. You may want connection, conversation and closeness and your partner may need some "Me" time, some unplug time to digest whatever they are going through or simply their day. It is helpful to try and take some time to ask yourself the question: why does my partner have this need? Perhaps pause to consider why they have a current need for "Me" time and get in the habit of discussing each other's needs, when they become clearer you can have a better understanding without taking it personally.

I know in my relationship it tends to be when there are a clash of needs which becomes the most difficult to navigate. I am a man who loves connection, I love to communicate and I love to feel a part of something, my need for alone time is very small compared to my partner's needs. A need is a need, so it's important that both are understood and both are met, sometimes it becomes a little messy when you both have a need which is opposite to the other. If I have a need for closeness at the same time my partner has a need for some time alone, you can see how if those needs are not met its going to cause a problem and sometimes it does, I want closeness at the exact moment my partner wants space, both are valid and legitimate needs, trying to navigate that is not always easy and even now it's something which can still cause each of us fractures. You just have to keep talking it through, keep trying to meet the need of your partner while at the same time not neglecting your own need, because if you neglect your own need over and over again you are going to start to become bitter.

I have often said pick your battles wisely, relationships are all about give and take, they are also about compromise and meeting halfway and sometimes you have to be prepared to not get what you want from time to time in order to give your partner what they want time to time.

Chapter 33 - The Beautiful Difference Between A Man and A Woman

I am going to try my level best to communicate as clearly and as concisely as possible on this topic, in the hope I don't start World War Three. I do believe it's an important topic to mention and I have given thought to what I am about to write for some time. My heart is really to educate on this matter because there have been two spectrums of thought when it comes to equality and both for me are not right. On the one hand we have men being paid more than women for the same job and on the other we have extreme feminists who now believe they don't need the male species in their life. For me, both are wrong.

So before you shoot me down, I am going to say what I feel and then do my best to explain it but before I do, let me make one thing clear. I do not believe for one moment it is right that if a man and woman do the same job that they should be paid differently, that kind of equality I am all for, if the job is like-for-like then the pay should be like-for-like, in some things for example tennis, a man plays three sets and a woman two, so if in the world of tennis women players want the same pay then they need to be playing three sets rather than two.

Now I am just going to say what I really feel and believe, please read this whole chapter before you jump to all conclusions and start tweeting me complaining and shouting me down. Men and women are not equal, there I said it. We are not equal; we are beautifully different. Male is not better than female and female is not better than male, neither sex has more value but a different currency. Some things in this life are stereotypical. However there are always some exceptions since we are all uniquely made, but the true hard reality is that there are some things in this world which women are far better at than men and there is also truth that men are far better than women at some things and instead of trying to be equal, if we just accepted that fact and then worked tirelessly to let the woman be the woman and the man be the man we would find harmony and beauty and most importantly the world would find order and our homes would find peace.

I know first-hand that when my girl experiences me in my masculine energy it encourages her to express her feminine energy and both are needed and important to find peace and excitement. So for a man to tap into his masculine energy that may look like him being gentlemanly, courteous and romantic, it may look like him providing for her and protecting her in some way, sweet gestures like opening the door or reassuring her when she is afraid are small little expressions of masculine energy, feminine energy may look at expressions of affection, kindness and gentleness, the woman may wear a dress, put on makeup.... Both are needed to bring the two of them together.

Sadly, now we live in a world where men can't be men because women see it as weakness or a lack on their part. A few years back I witnessed a group of about eight women standing in the car park watching one of their girlfriends trying to park the car, a man went over to the woman and asked if he could help her, the woman agreed but half of her friends were enraged that she was allowing a man to park her car and tried to intervene and park the car themselves. What a sad sad story, the man wasn't trying to insult the woman, in fact he was being a gentleman and asking if he could help, he wasn't asking because he felt it was a chance to make the woman appear to be inferior to him and yet the eight women were in an argument with each other and felt threatened and devalued by such an act. It honestly made my heart drop. Women don't stop a man from being a man and men don't stop women from being a woman, we are beautifully different.

I am so thankful I am in a relationship with a woman who is totally aligned with me on this very point, we do have arguments and disagreements but never about this, we know what we both have to offer each other and I am not going to fight for equality when in reality she is better at some things than I, not all of that is going to be down to the difference between man and woman but it's something that needs looking at in our world we live in. I am encouraging men to be men and not all men are good at being masculine or indeed being what a woman needs, sometimes the way we talk to women and about them has no connection with being masculine, may I say it, that if as men we can tap into our masculine energy more, then we may well find that the women around us start treating us the way we really want to be treated.

Masculine energy described from

masculinedevelopment.com is seen as active and assertive. It knows where it's going, and takes action to get there. Masculinity does not receive, but rather it goes forth. Masculine energy influences its environment, not the other way around. Masculine energy is very clear in its intentions – there is never a doubt in its mind.

Looking at this definition you can see the confidence in being masculine. I love the part where it says it does not receive but rather it goes forth. It gives of itself, it leads the way, it reassures and is full of direction and poise. Men we need to go forth, we need to give, we need to lead and we need to provide a sense of freedom for a woman to be who she wants to be.

It's important to look at the feminine energy too. From thefeminewoman.com feminine energy is described as the energy of life within you. It is an energy of ever-changing flow. It responds to emotion in relationships and seeks to feel and experience love. The feminine energy is similar to the energy of the ocean.

You can see from the descriptions that both energies are very much different but how they encourage each other. Men we need to be masculine, if you don't know what that looks like for you do some research on it, for the few women who may read this book please tap into your feminine energy, however I do believe that men should take the lead and in doing so your feminine energy is expressed and increased.

So I don't believe in equality with regards to how we are built, we are beautifully different, no sex is greater or more valuable, just different. We don't need chauvinists and we don't need feminists, we need each other.

It is going to be invaluable to encourage each other in your respective energies, affirm, approve and encourage the positive traits you see and witness in your partner, each time we call out something we love, see and admire, we actually strengthen our bond and encourage our partner to continue expressing and manifesting the positive energy which actually builds attraction. I have come to know first-hand that if a woman feels more feminine she tends to build up that attraction with you, it just continually grows in the right environment and culture of such a dynamic energy that it becomes a self-sufficient supply of good energy and ridiculous amounts of attraction.

It is worth noting the notion that when it comes to how a man and woman are stimulated the man has been compared to the microwave and the woman the oven. Like a microwave, it fires quickly, it heats quickly and some minutes later in most cases it's done the job it's needed to. It's a fairly instant heat source, it fires quickly but doesn't generally have the stamina, society has drawn comparisons to the way a man can tap into that instant energy of intimacy or passion and then once expressed its desire and passion can quickly be released and diminish, on the contrary for women, they have been compared to an oven, they take longer to heat up, they take longer to get into that frame of intimacy and desire and yet once they've reached that point of intimacy and desire they stay in that place much longer than a man, an oven takes time to cool down, a microwave once it's done its job tends to cool rapidly and after about five minutes you never knew it had even been used.

This is the way we are made, it's not right or wrong, but it is helpful to remember the different mechanics of both a man and a woman, knowing how each other operates and responds should help both of us, as men to be more mindful of the stages and the scene which needs to be set in order for a woman to enter into that place of intimacy and for women to know how quickly men can go from something ordinary to very quickly being in a place of desire and passion, knowing the feminine and masculine energy will help you with your partner establish a clearer understanding which is going to need patience from both sides.

I do find it fascinating that men and women are so different in this area and objectively you can see where misunderstanding and hurt can manifest if you don't know the differences. Another interesting reflection is men often feel loved through the power of lovemaking and sex, we tend to express intimacy which in turn promotes love, the interesting thing for most women is that they actually need to feel loved, valued and secure in order to be intimate and make love. Men feel it by doing and women do after they feel. So it is important that as a couple you grasp the mechanics otherwise you could both get hurt, be misunderstood and both of you could end up with your needs not met.

If the woman doesn't experience the buildup through kind thoughts, nice gestures, and you being in your masculine energy which makes your woman feel safe and secure, we all run the risk of our woman withdrawing and taking a step back and when that happens, it can cause all sorts of other secondary problems and we don't want that.

I know as a man it can be frustrating at the time and effort and mindfulness we need to show in order for our woman to get to the space and energy where they desire intimacy and yet by our own admission as men, we don't need all day to be wowed, we need merely a minute, a touch of a hand, a kiss on the lips and we can get into that place much more readily. Even so, despite it seemingly appearing unfair, your woman is worth it and if you feel she isn't you're probably with the wrong woman.

Chapter 34 - Romantic Love and Ambience

I think its befitting to end this book with the essence of romance. Whether you're in a relationship or just started one or waiting to enter one, it's important to leave you all with an impression of hope and to celebrate your growth, enlightenment and re-framing to take the knowledge shared in this book and apply it to your life in your current relationship or in the one to come.

I have always been a romantic, how much that grows or is expressed often comes at the strength and indeed the response of the one I am showing romance too. Romance is the most beautiful of things. It's a celebration of your love and affection that you have between yourselves. Romance for me is often first found in my thoughts and then executed in expression and action. I get happy and energised preparing thoughtful surprises, gifts and expressions way before I actually bring them to fruition. If I have organised a romantic weekend away I get so happy even before the actual event.

As men we need to initiate romance, we need to set the scene, be sweet in thought and gesture, open the car door, put on her coat, compliment her beauty but more importantly her intelligence, a woman is always intelligent if she is your woman, she is smart enough to know you're a good catch. It's an important comment to make and something many men fall down on. Too often men expect and push for the physical intimacy of a woman, but first intimacy must be created in the mind and the heart before it's expressed in the body. I know I have a role to play if I want to create the ambience of intimacy. Make love to a woman's mind and making love to the body will flow out of that.

Me and my girl love to dress up, we even have home dates, we sometimes cook for each other or at times like Valentine's Day we end up cooking together, it's a beautiful celebration which we both equally enjoy and are often the happiest memories we recollect when we discuss the things we have done as a couple. We both love getting dressed up, especially for the other person. That always means a lot when my girl dresses up for me, it makes me happy and sets the scene of romance.

Romance is an important part of a successful relationship. The excitement between two individuals is breathtaking and warming, we can actually crave it like we crave a cold drink on a very hot day. Romance offers mystery, it keeps us curious, it keeps us exploring each other, it makes us go deeper and deeper. It's like the ocean, it's vast and it never seems to have an end. It's a celebration of your devotion, love and affection, it's not pushy or cheesy, it's not a sign of weakness, it's a sign of a beautiful maturity to explore the other in such a pure and innocent way.

I have encouraged you as a man to express your emotions and most importantly own them, whether they are good or bad, they need to find expression, romance is an emotion of love, it's also an expression of attraction towards another person. Romance is a good thing and my girl loves it.

It takes the right ambience and setting to encourage and sharpen the effectiveness of romance in your relationship. Sometimes it's a specific event other times it's a series of gestures. The setting of a romantic mood is essential, so a weekend away is ideal, it's a change of environment and setting which enables you to both relax and enjoy your surroundings and each other. Romance is what takes my girl from the position of best friend to lover. We must be mindful and thoughtful in setting the scene. You can do the same action but get a different result depending on where the action takes place, some things need to be done in private and others in public. If I present flowers to my girl in private I get one outcome and if I present her flowers publicly I get another. It's sometimes good to experiment but be mindful each girl is different and you know best, some gestures may cause great pride and love and others embarrassment and maybe even shame.

I have always enjoyed other people's expressions of love. Stephen Chapmans' book about the five love languages is something which has been hugely insightful, if you've never read that book, it's well worth purchasing and pondering over what is expressed. The five love languages which Chapman expresses are words of affirmation, gift giving, quality time, physical touch and acts of service. We all have a primary love language and a secondary one. Typically for most men our top two love languages are physical touch and words of affirmation. It's important to find out what your love language is as we often express love the way we want to receive it, the difficulty is, often women don't have the same two as men, often some have one, typically physical touch is normally in the top two for most human beings but there are many exemptions.

Knowing your love language and your partner's is extremely helpful and liberating in knowing how to connect. It is a fascinating topic but could also reveal some of your frustrations and explain why that despite your best effort there often feels like a disconnect between you and your partner. I know at times this has been true of all my romantic relationships. The interesting thing here is it's always easy to meet the need of another when you have that need yourself. It's far more difficult to meet the need of another when you don't have that particular need yourself.

It also provides a problem that if you believe there is only two ways to love you, you may miss out on real expressions of love because you only believe in physical touch and words of affirmation, so if your partner buys you a gift, you may still like it and appreciate it, but it won't convert into "My partner loves me." It's also true of your partners experience, you may get into a fight with your partner and they may say something like "Hey, you really don't love me" and our response maybe something like "I do love you, I hug you and I tell you I love and appreciate you" and yet if your partner's love language is quality time and acts of service, they actually might not feel loved because while you tell them and you hug them, you don't cook them dinner, you don't put away your phone. It's something really we should all look at, for the benefit of you, your partner and your relationship.

Having an open communication to when and how we feel loved is important to make sure there is not a disconnect but a continual flow where both of you in your relationship feel loved and sometimes that takes time. I often joke and say "I can feel loved in 2 minutes." Hug me and kiss me and tell me you love me and I am good to go, the most frustrating is when you have a partner who needs you to cook them dinner, run them a bath, wash the dishes, take out the trash etc. and after all those eight hours of action they then feel loved the way you and I did in two minutes, but that's love and it's not always easy to express it and then keep it!

Outside of communication and knowing your love language, scheduling time to have a weekly date night is essential, it's like blood supply, it needs a regular flow of blood to keep it going, to keep it alive and it has to be non-negotiable. Not having babysitters is not an excuse, find a couple with kids and offer to look after their kids so they can then look after yours. Forget the excuses, your relationship can't afford to not have time invested in it. Spontaneous is good but when it comes to a date night, I would pick a day of the week and stick to it religiously. During this date I would just encourage you both to be, to enjoy each other's company and have fun, remind your partner of what you like in them and show gratitude to what you love and are appreciative about who they are and what they do for you.

I encourage you all as men to take the first step, to be brave and be a man, be romantic, create a safe environment, study the love languages, know your love language, communicate it with your partner and have them communicate theirs with you too. Take the initiative and schedule a date night and start telling them what you love and appreciate.

Any true "Mark of a man" actions should be ones which improve the state of mind and mood of another. As men it's time we use the beautiful expression of romance to create a gorgeous and inviting environment where our partner thrives and blossoms. The excitement and love which can be jointly experienced is one of the wonders of the world.